"I'll Never Lie to You"

JIMMY CARTER IN HIS OWN WORDS

"I'll Never Lie to You"

JIMMY CARTER IN HIS OWN WORDS

Robert L. Turner

BALLANTINE BOOKS • NEW YORK

ISBN 0-345-25702-2-175

Manufactured in the United States of America

First Edition: September 1976

TO OTILE

Foreword

Jimmy Carter is not an easy man to understand. He rarely puts his instincts or emotions or motivations on display.

But he is an intriguing figure, a man with an unlikely blend of heritage, politics and religion; a man whose startling success tells us as much about the nation as about himself; a man who is clearly worth understanding—who has become required study, in fact.

This book grew out of the conviction that the best place to look is Carter's own words, not only the memorized speeches and position papers of the campaign, but also the impromptu sermons and philosophy, the occasional contradictions and changes of tone, and the offhand, private remarks which have surfaced from time to time.

Carter himself contends that he is very cautious about what he says. But from the time I first covered him in December, 1975, I have increasingly found his

remarks thought-provoking—and surprisingly reveal-
ing.

My wife, Otile McManus, with Carter quotes swirl-
ing about her ankles, has contributed to this book in
tangible and intangible ways beyond measure, and
for this I am grateful beyond expression.

I was also buoyed by the support of *The Boston
Globe,* and particularly by encouragement and help
from Curtis Wilkie, Matt Storin, Marty Nolan and
Tom Winship. Thank you all.

A sincere effort was made to acknowledge all
quotations not made publically, or to me personally.

Robert L. Turner

1

Running

VERY EARLY

"Hello, Bobby. I'm Jimmy Carter, and I'm going to be your next president. And I'm going to be a wonderful president."

—November, 1975, meeting the
son of a campaign
supporter

SOBERING

"For me, as for you or for any person, the prospect of being president of the United States is a sobering thought, one that calls more for humility than for pride, more for reflection than for celebration."

—May 28, 1976, Ohio

SPECIAL YEAR

"This year is going to be very special in my life, and I think in your life."

—January 22, 1976, Washington; remarks to the board of the Urban Coalition

RUNNING

"The main difficulty I had to overcome was embarrassment, telling folks I was running for—you know, for president."

—late 1974; interview

FEAR

(Does the idea of being president scare you at all?)
"No. I know that I can be a good president."
(Have you ever been afraid?)
"No."
(Never?)
"Not in the sense of the word fear. There have been four or five times when I faced the possibility of death. I know enough about myself that I wasn't afraid. Once, on a submarine in the spring of 1949, I was officer of the deck . . . and we were caught in a storm. I was swept off by a huge wave. I could have disappeared in the ocean and no one would have noticed. But I didn't. I survived. I'm a fatalist, I guess."

—February 27, 1976; Boston interview

3

PRIORITIES

". . . the campaign experience and the wide-ranging affinity I have with these groups—blacks, unions, farmers, businessmen, I think I know very clearly and certainly, or will when the campaign is over, the order of priority of their concerns. It will be up to me as president to determine the priorities among groups. I don't have any fear about my ability to do that."

—March 16, 1976, Washington;
interview

DECIDING TO RUN

"I started comparing my own experience and knowledge of government with the candidates, not against 'the presidency' and not against Thomas Jefferson and George Washington. It made it a whole lot easier."

—late 1974; interview

HALF AND HALF

"I think that anybody who aspires to higher office such as the presidency would have to have a high opinion of themselves. I think probably politicians are about half ego and about half humility. I think I have my share of both of them."

—April 11, 1975, Little Rock;
press conference

4

DOUBTS

(Do you have any doubts? About yourself, about God, about life?)

"I can't think of any. I, obviously, don't know all the answers to philosophical questions and theological questions—the kind of questions that are contrived. But the things that I haven't been able to answer in a theory or a supposition, I just accept them and go on—things that I can't influence or change.

"I do have, obviously, many doubts about the best way to answer a question. Or to alleviate a concern. Or how to meet a need, or how to create in my own life a more meaningful purpose, and to let my life be expanded, in my heart and mind. So doubts about the best avenue to take among many options is a kind of doubt that is a constant presence with me.

"But doubt about my faith? No. Doubts about my purpose of life? I don't have any doubts about that."

—May 6, 1976; television interview

APPROVAL

Carter described a campaign trip to Berlin, N.H., in the winter, and a talk he gave there to a group of 6-, 7- and 8-year-olds in a tiny schoolhouse. He said he asked the children if they knew what the president was, then ended by telling them to talk to their parents so he could win all the votes in Berlin and in New Hampshire and in Disney World. The children loved it, Carter said.

"They just mobbed me. They ran up and grabbed

my legs, my hands—they wanted to touch me. It really makes me feel good."

—February 21, 1976, Worcester, Mass.; interview

WINNING

"I've never been more determined in my life to win anything, not because I just want to be president but because I honestly believe in the bottom of my soul that I can represent what our people are and what we want to be and what we can be."

—March 11, 1976, Chicago; speech at the Monument of Faith Evangelistic Church

"I don't have to be governor. That is not the most important thing to me."

—June, 1970, Atlanta; interview

"It's very important for me to win. But it's not the most important thing in my life."

—December 9, 1975, Medford, Mass.; speech to college students

"There's a certain sense of security and equanimity that comes from a deep religious faith. But I don't intend to lose."

—February 21, 1976, Worcester, Mass.; interview

LOSING

"I was going through a stage in my life there that was a very difficult one. I had run for governor and lost. Everything I did was not gratifying. When I succeeded in something, I got no pleasure out of it. When I failed at something, it was a horrible experience for me."

—May 6, 1976; television interview

SHOW ME

"You show me a good loser and I will show you a loser."

—1975, from Carter's autobiography, *Why Not the Best?*

WON-LOSS RECORD

In the Navy, as a pitcher for his submarine baseball team . . .

"I honestly don't remember too much about how I did, won-loss wise. It didn't seem important. Playing was the only thing that mattered."

—February, 1971, Atlanta

NEW HAMPSHIRE

"Either me or one of my family tried to shake hands with almost every Democrat in the state. This is an image that I've created."

> —February 25, 1976 (the day after his New Hampshire victory) Boston; press conference

"The other candidates stand on the corner in the snow while the TV cameras are on. Then they go get warm. We don't. We campaign all day every day."

> —February, 1976

THE LIBERALS

"I thought one of the liberal candidates would emerge from New Hampshire and Massachusetts. That none did is one of the most unpredictable things that have happened. No clear challenger to me has been identified. We'll have to wait and see about that for the next six or seven states. Meantime, we'll be winning and accumulating delegates."

> —March 11, 1976, Chicago; interview

UNACCUSTOMED AS I AM . . .

"I could have left them in such a state they'd still be applauding. It's easy enough to do. You pause at just the right points, end a sentence on an upbeat note. But I don't do that. . . .

8

"I like to see the audience's intensity of concentration, their lack of movement and coughing. It doesn't matter to me whether they applaud hysterically. That kind of enthusiasm can evaporate right after the speech."

—May, 1976, Baltimore;
interview

PEANUT POWER

"How many of you know how to use the telephone? [chorus of yes-es.] Okay, very good. You got uncles and aunts and grandmothers and grandfathers and big brothers and sisters over 18 years old. You can all call and ask them to vote for Jimmy Carter."

—March, 1976, Wisconsin; conversation
with school children

INVITATION

"When I get in the White House, I don't want you to leave me there all by myself. . . . I'll be there at the front door wating for you."

—February 10, 1976, Manchester,
N.H.; to a group of elderly
persons

THE FLOCK

"We've accumulated literally thousands of fervent supporters who'll do literally anything for me. . . .

9

"I feel a heavy responsibility on my shoulders. I would die first—not to disappoint them in any way."

—February 21, 1976, Worcester, Mass.; interview

FACTORY GATES

"On a factory shift line. . . . everybody that comes through there, when I shake hands with them, for that instance, for that instant, I really care about in a genuine way. And I believe they know it quite a lot of times. Quite often I will shake hands with women who work in a plant, and I just touch their hands, and quite frequently they'll put their arms around my neck and say, 'God bless you, son' or 'Good luck—I'll help you and good luck.' "

—May 6, 1976; television interview

IF . . .

"If I'm elected and if I live, the executive branch of the government will be reorganized. . . ."

—February 27, 1976, Salem, Mass.; speech to college students

THE PRESS

"I feel good about the press. I think the press has treated me well. And I would not be where I am now had the press not accommodated some of my errors and asked me a second question rather than quoting a ridiculous answer I may have made."

—May 2, 1976; airborne interview

TO THE REPORTERS . . .

"You've treated me very well so far."
(Compared to what?)
"To the way you treated Nixon."

—June, 1976, Ohio; on the press bus

THOMAS DEWEY

"Dewey went around so long acting like he was president that the people thought it was time for a change. . . . I don't want that to happen to me."

—June 29, 1976, Milwaukee; mayors' conference

PRESSING THE . . .

(After mistakenly shaking the hand of a department-store mannequin . . .)
"Better give her a brochure, too."

—April, 1976, Columbus, Ohio

2

Plains, Georgia

PLAINS GEORGIA

"I am a Southerner and an American."

—1975; from Carter's
autobiography,
Why Not the Best?

POOR

"My daddy's people have lived here in Georgia for 210 years. I come from one of the poorest parts of the country. In my county we don't have a doctor, we don't have a pharmacist, a dentist. . . .

—March, 1976, Florida;
speech

4 A.M.

"I'm the first child in my daddy's family who ever had a chance. . . . I used to get up at four in the morning to pick peanuts. Then I'd walk three miles along the railroad track to deliver them. My house had no running water or electricity."

—December, 1975, Jackson, Miss.;
talking to high school students

TENNIS

". . . adjacent to our house, between the house and store, we had a tennis court on our farm."

—1975; from Carter's autobiography,
Why Not the Best?

THE OLD SUBMARINER

(Questioned about his decision to order a tennis court and swimming pool for the governor's mansion only weeks after he moved in in 1971 . . .)
"I need some place where I can relax. And actually I can think better at the bottom of a swimming pool than I can at some other places."

—May 5, 1971, Atlanta

BAREFOOT BOY

"I remember as a barefooted child the intense fear that I had of rabies when mad dogs who were not vaccinated would run through the streets on occasion. I remember very distinctly that when anyone was afflicted with pneumonia, and particularly the horrible expression—double pneumonia, the prospects for survival were very dismal. Whooping cough and measles and mumps could be fatal. Smallpox was rarely known, but typhoid was a constant threat. Typhus fever was something always before us. The dread and constant name of polio was frequently mentioned in the families of that day. These are almost ancient, historic names for medical afflictions."

—May 10, 1974, Georgia; speech to the Governor's Conference on Education

SLING SHOT

"I remember when I was a child, I lived on a farm about three miles from Plains, and we didn't have electricity or running water. We lived on the railroad—Seaboard Coastline Railroad. Like all farm boys I had a flip—a sling shot. They had stabilized the railroad bed with little, white, round rocks, which I used for ammunition. I would go out frequently to the railroad and gather the most perfectly shaped rocks of proper size. I always had a few in my pockets, and I had others cached away around the farm, so that they would be convenient if I ran out of my pocket supply.

"One day I was leaving the railroad track with my pockets full of rocks and hands full of rocks, and my mother came out on the front porch—this is not a very interesting story but it illustrates a point—and she had in her hands a plate full of cookies that she had just backed for me. She called me, I am sure with love in

16

her heart, and said, 'Jimmy, I've baked some cookies for you.' I remember very distinctly walking up to her and standing there for 15 or 20 seconds, in honest doubt about whether I should drop those rocks—which were worthless—and take the cookies that my mother had prepared for me, which between her and me were very valuable."

—May 4, 1974, Athens, Ga.;
Georgia Law Day speech

BOILED PEANUTS

"Every year when the peanuts got ripe, I'd go out into the field in the afternoon with a little homemade wagon and I would cull the peanuts up out of the ground, take them back to the yard and pump water and pick off the peanuts and wash them, and put them in brine, and I would get up very early the next morning, boil those peanuts, put them in about 20 little bags.

"I had a wicker basket, and I would walk down the railroad track about 3 miles to Plains, Georgia, to sell my peanuts. Plains is now and was then a town of about 550 people. It was my first experience with metropolitan life. And very early I was able—six or seven years old—to judge very accurately who the good people were on the streets of Plains and who the bad people were.

"The good people were the ones that bought boiled peanuts. The bad ones didn't.

"So I haven't come any further in my ability to judge others, but today I want to talk about judgment to you."

—April 16, 1975, Misenheimer, N.C.;
speech to college students

SPORTS FAN

"I couldn't throw it hard enough—it didn't hum—to be a good baseball pitcher. And I was never tall enough to really do well in basketball. Since I grew up around the swamps, I mostly hunted and fished when I was a youngster.

"But I've always been one of the biggest sports fans in the world.

"I did play a little basketball at Plains High School, though, and ran a little track. . . . After I got to Annapolis, I was on the cross-country team."

—February, 1971, Atlanta

TOOTH DELAY

"Some of the physical requirements listed in the catalogue (for Annapolis) gave me deep concern. 'Malocclusion of teeth' was my biggest theoretical problem. When I ate fruit, the knowledge that my teeth did not perfectly meet interfered with my enjoying the flavor."

—1975; from Carter's autobiography, *Why Not the Best?*

WAR AND PEACE

"When I was 12 years old I liked to read, and I had a school principal, named Miss Julia Coleman—Judge Marshall (a local judge) knows her. She forced me pretty much to read, read, read classical books.

She would give me a gold star when I read ten and a silver star when I read five.

"One day, she called me in and said, 'Jimmy, I think it's time for you to read *War and Peace*.' I was completely relieved because I thought it was a book about cowboys and Indians.

"Well, I went to the library and checked it out, and it was 1415 pages thick, I think, written by Tolstoy, as you know, about Napoleon's entry into Russia in the 1812–1815 era. He had never been defeated and he was sure he could win, but he underestimated the severity of the Russian winter and the peasants' love for their land.

"To make a long story short, the next spring he retreated in defeat. The course of history was changed; it probably affected our own lives.

"The point of the book is, and what Tolstoy points out in the epilogue is, that he didn't write the book about Napoleon or the czar of Russia or even the generals, except in a rare occasion. He wrote it about the students and the housewives and the barbers and the farmers and the privates in the Army. And the point of the book is that the course of human events, even the greatest historical events, are not determined by the leaders of a nation or a state, like presidents or governors or senators. They are controlled by the combine wisdom and courage and commitment and discernment and unselfishness and compassion and love and idealism of the common ordinary people. If that was true in the case of Russia where they had a czar or France where they had an emperor, how much more true is it in our own case where the Constitution charges us with a direct responsibility for determining what our government is and ought to be?"

—May 4, 1974, Athens, Ga.;
Georgia Law Day speech

19

MY PEOPLE

"I do have unique experience. One of the strongest and best of these is my relationship with poor people. That's where I came from. That's where I lived. Those are my people. Not only whites but particularly blacks. And it's not an accident that (Cong.) Andy Young and Daddy King support me. They know that I understand their problems. They know that I've demonstrated an eagerness to solve them."

—June 14, 1976, airborne interview

BLACK FRIENDS

"They care for me and I care for them. We have a lot in common, a belief in one another. We share a common faith in Christ. We speak the same language. We sing the same hymns. We've seen the same poverty and the same disease. We've seen the same struggles in the South and the same growth. We've overcome the same obstacles. It has bound us together in the spirit of brotherhood and love."

—April, 1976, Indianapolis; speech in a black church

DADDY

"Somebody came out the other day and talked to my mother and asked her, 'How does it feel to have been married to a racist?' Well, you know, if my Daddy was still living he would be part of the modern enlightened consciousness between black and white people. He died in 1953. Even the black people who lived at home never thought about, you know, equality and riding in the front of the bus and going to the same school as whites."

—June 14, 1976, airborne
interview

NO COLOR LINE

"(My mother) was registered nurse, She would work 12 hours a day or 20 hours a day and then come home and care for her family and minister to the people of our little community, both black and white.

"My mother knew no color line. Her black friends were just as welcome in our home as her white friends, a fact that shocked some people, sometimes even my father, who was very conventional then in his views on race."

—June 1, 1976, Los Angeles;
speech at the Martin Luther
King Hospital

MOTHER

"My mother, who is now 76 years old, is a registered nurse and joined the Peace Corps in 1966 at age 68. She served for two years in a small hospital in a remote village in India. It saddens me to know that because of job discrimination against older people in the United States, my mother's service to India would have been almost impossible in her own country."

—January 26, 1976; position paper

21

FARM BOY

"When I grew up on the farm and when I got hurt, my mamma and daddy were always there—on the edge of the field or not too far from the creek. If I got thrown off a mule, my daddy was close by to pick me up. But my children and I aren't always in the same place. In this modern world with all the automobiles and everybody in the family spread all around, you don't have that stability or assurance and that constant presence to help you when you need guidance or when you get hurt."

—April, 1976, Indianapolis; speech in a black church

SUCKER FISH

"One of the exciting times of the year was when the redhorse sucker fish were running. . . . The suckers were fearsome fighters, and the meat was delicious if slashed in thin strips so that the tiny bones could be thoroughly cooked. Although there are still these fish, suckers, in the large creeks, the many dams on our main rivers now make this ocean-to-headwater annual pilgrimage impossible."

—1975, from Carter's autobiography, *Why Not the Best?*

DAMS

"We ought to get the Army Corps of Engineers out of the dam business. I personally believe that we have built enough dams in this country and will be extremely reluctant as president to build any more. At a time

22

when the whole country is concerned about inflation and high taxes, we don't need to spend tens of millions of dollars for the purpose of perpetuating the Army Corps of Engineers."

—early 1976, Hanover, N.H.;
prepared statement

NO SWEETHEART

"There were two or three girls that I liked from time to time in high school and college. But I never had any real sweetheart, and in fact never told any girl that I loved her."

—1975, from Carter's autobiography, *Why Not the Best?*

ENSIGN

"My ensign's salary was $300 per month, out of which we paid $100 for rent, $54 for my food on the ship, and $75 for a war bond. That left $71 for all other expenses in a month's time. Rosalynn has always handled responsibility well. She has a strong will of her own (which has seemed to get stronger with each passing year)."

—1975, from Carter's autobiography, *Why Not the Best?*

THE NAVY

"You only have one life and I began to wonder if I should spend mine engaged in war, even if I could rationalize it as the prevention of war."

—late 1975; interview

A JOKE

(Explaining why there is a large gap between the ages of his three grown sons and of his young daughter . . .)

"My wife and I had an argument for 14 years . . . which I finally won."

—May 25, 1976, Warren, R.I.; rally

AMY

"I have always loved children; I wish Rosalynn and I had ten of them. Yet, after we returned to Plains from the Navy, we found that Rosalynn had some physical problems which prevented her from having another child. It was more than a dozen years later when an operation became necessary to remove a large tumor from her uterus. After that operation, Rosalynn's obstetrician said that she could have another child. We began to pray for a daughter.

"Amy came."

—1975, from Carter's autobiography, *Why Not the Best?*

ONCE IN LOVE WITH . . .

"My mother is a registered nurse and when we grew up on the farm she was always a dominant factor in our family. . . . You might think that she was the most dominant female factor in my life but that is not true because my wife Rosalynn, whom I married a little more than 25 years ago and whom I love more now that I did when I married her, and who helped me in 1970 to personally visit, look in the eye, talk to, meet and ask for the help of more than six hundred thousand Georgians. . . . You might think that she was the most dominant female in my life, but that is not true. . . . We now have a four-year-old daughter named Amy. And Amy is the female dominant factor in my life."

—May 1, 1972, Georgia; speech to the League of Women Voters

ALWAYS IN LOVE WITH . . .

"She (Amy) didn't learn to read until she was in the first grade about three months ago, and now she has read twenty-five books, and she feels that this is the most important thing in her life. Recently there was a headline picture on the sports page of the Atlanta morning newspaper with me as Governor representing the state and the legislators who were visiting the Atlanta Hawks basketball game. And Amy was sitting in my lap reading a book and the title of the photograph was 'Did Winnie the Pooh Win?' "

—February 13, 1974, Georgia; speech at the Tristate Winter Conference

FAMILY

"I've got a good family. I hope that you'll be part of my family."

—February 10, 1976, Manchester, N.H.; to a group of elderly persons

DEMOCRAT

"I've always been a Democrat ever since I was eight years old. When the convention was going on I used to go out to the car in the middle of the night and hook up the battery radio into the battery of the car to see who was going to be our nominee. I felt very remote from the selection process on a farm about three miles west of Plains."

> —July 10, 1971, Atlanta; speech to Democratic Committee Meeting

SOUTHERN POLITICIANS

". . . One of the greatest afflictions on the South in the past . . . is that in many instances politicians have underestimated the southern people. This has caused, I think, in a great measure, the lack of objectivity and accurate analysis of the quality of the South and its people and its institutions by the rest of the nation and the world."

> —April 30, 1971, Georgia; speech at Emory University

REUNION

"We have three sons and an eight-year-old daughter, Amy. I am semiretired. My family is in the lemonade business (Amy had a soft drink stand). I have one grandson, Jason, born in August. He can already walk and say 14 words. He's the finest grandchild ever born in Georgia."

> —June, 1976, Americus, Ga.; introducing himself to his Plains High School classmates

COUNTRY RADIO

"During a recent country radio discussion of a new so-called sunshine law—one that requires open governmental meetings—a caller said to me: 'There are two things a person should never watch being made. One is potted meat and the other is law.' "

—August 12, 1974; column by Carter in *The New York Times*

MY CUSTOMERS

"I have customers that I really care for and love. If one of my customers gets sick or his wife gets sick, I go by the hospital to see him. I send flowers. I even offer to take care of the children.

"But when I hire a lobbyist to go to Washington or Atlanta to represent me, that lobbyist doesn't care anything about my farmer customers."

—April 16, 1975, Misenheimer, N.C.; speech to college students

GEORGIANS

"Throughout this entire year and all during last year, I had a tremendous advantage over all my opponents and that was my Georgia people who had confidence in me."

—May 4, 1976, Atlanta; speech to supporters

PLAINS, GEORGIA

"It's just like the South Sea Islands there in its distance from politics. I put on my work clothes and nobody defers to me."

—February 21, 1976, Worcester, Mass.; interview

3

Georgia, U.S.A.

I AM . . .

"I am a farmer, an engineer, a businessman, a planner, a scientist, a governor and a Christian."

> —December 13, 1974, Washington; announcing his candidacy for president

"I am a businessman and a Christian. I am a father and a Christian. I am a politician and a Christian. I am a governor and a Christian.

"I have been a better businessman, father, politician and governor than I am a Christian, because in my secular positions I have never been satisfied with mediocrity. I am, at best, a mediocre Christian. It is obvious that in these present times, as Christians we need to recognize frankly our own inadequacies and failures, ask God's forgiveness, and commit ourselves to a standard of perfection."

> —May 11, 1974, Detroit; speech to Christian Businessmen's Committee

"I am an engineer, I am a conservationist, and I am a scientist, an environmentalist; I am a nuclear physicist, I am an outdoors man, I am a Christian, and I don't see any conflict among these things."

> —March 15, 1975, Pittsburgh; speech to the National Wildlife Federation

AMBITION

(Carter said he had not always wanted to be president . . .)
"When I was at Annapolis, the only thing I wanted to be was chief of naval operations."

> —April, 1976, Green Bay, Wisc.; rally

LABELS

Carter described himself as "fairly liberal" on civil rights, social justice and the environment, and "quite conservative" on balanced budgets and long-range planning.

—March 12, 1975, New York; interview

Carter described himself as "the only true conservative" in the 1970 Georgia governor's race.

—1970

REDNECK

In the 1970 campaign, Carter called himself "basically a redneck." He also said:

"I expect to have particularly strong support from the people who voted for George Wallace for president and the ones who voted for Lester Maddox."

He also claimed "excellent support" from the NAACP and black churchmen.

—June, 1970, Atlanta; interview

A LETTER—DISPUTED

"I have never had anything but the highest praise for Governor Wallace. My support for Senator Jackson (at the 1972 convention) was based upon a personal request from our late Senator Richard Russell shortly before his death. I think you will find that Senator Jackson, Governor Wallace and I are in close agreement on most issues.

Let me ask you to consider one other factor before I close. There are times when two men working toward the same end can accomplish more if they are not completely tied together. I think you will find that Governor Wallace understands this.

Please let me know when I can be of service to you or your children in Atlanta. I hope I have been able to give you a slightly better impression of me."

> —August 4, 1972, Atlanta; letter to constitutent. Carter's press secretary, Jody Powell, has said that he wrote the letter and Carter never saw it.

STEVEN BRILL

(Brill, who wrote a partially negative story, "Jimmy Carter's Pathetic Lies," in *Harper's Magazine* . . .)

". . . completely misquoted me and also misquoted eight others. . . . The whole article . . . was grossly distorted."

> —February 27, 1976, Salem, Mass.; speech to college students

TALKING DOWN

"I don't know if anyone from my part of the country can please some people up North—the ones who cheered me when I took on George Wallace, but then walked away shaking their heads and upset with this or that after I beat Wallace. In order to win against Wallace, in the South and in the North, I had to speak to supporters in a way they could understand and respond to. It's not in me to talk down to people, to give them lectures, to make them feel like they're below others and they're the only ones who make mistakes or don't have charity in their hearts. I did my best to

33

appeal to a lot of people who turned to George Wallace out of frustration and anger and confusion. I wasn't being 'evasive' with these people. I was talking straight to them, and I believe a lot of them heard me."

—1976; interview

COUNTERPRODUCTIVE

During the 1966 and 1970 campaigns for governor, ". . . if I'd gone in and said, 'All of you are wrong. You shouldn't have done what you did. I'm better than you are, it would have been a counterproductive thing. . . . I wouldn't have been elected. I wouldn't have gotten 10 percent of the votes.

"The point I'm making is that the South, including Georgia, has moved forward primarily because it hasn't been put in the position of having to renounce itself. You've got to give people credit for the progress they make and their change in attitudes."

—June 14, 1976, airborne interview

ACCEPTED

"I think I'm accepted, too, by the . . . conservative farmer-businessman who is not particularly committed to civil rights and human rights, but just wants to see the government run right. He wants to see it well-managed. I think I can do that."

—June 14, 1976, airborne interview

HOTCAKES

"Early one morning, immediately following my campaign, when I made my first foray into the rest of Georgia after becoming Governor, I went into a restaurant in southwest Georgia and I asked for an order of hotcakes and the girl in there brought me one little piece of butter. After I had finished about half the hotcakes, I called her over and I told her that if she didn't mind I'd like to have some more butter. She turned around and walked away and said, 'No.' I figured she didn't understand what I meant, so the next time she came by, which was a quite a while later, I said, 'Young lady, would you come over here a minute please; I'd like to have another pat of butter.' And, she said, 'No,' and she left again. Finally, I asked the security man who was with me to go get her and bringher back. When she walked over, I said, 'Listen, I don't want to make an issue of this, but I want some more butter.' She said 'You're not going to have it.' And, I said, 'Do you know who I am?' She said, 'Who?' And I said, 'I'm the Governor of Georgia.' She said, 'Do you know who I am?' I said, 'No.' She said, 'I'm the keeper of the butter.' "

—August 7, 1973, Athens, Ga.; speech to the Georgia Association of Colleges

A COMPLAINT

(In his 1970 race for governor against Carl Sanders, Carter said he was being treated unfairly by the Atlanta newspapers.)

"Sanders will make a speech and say we've got a terrible drug problem in the hippie district and that he's going to appoint a drug study panel. That's a bunch of bull—you know that. But damned if he won't get a quarter of a page in the *Atlanta Journal*."

—June, 1970, Atlanta; interview

THE REAL THING

"Since I've been in office, I have visited ten nations, and in each instance I've gone as the personal guest of the governments involved. I have met with the Presidents, Prime Ministers, Foreign Trade Officers, Cultural Exchange Officers, or others, and I have received treatment I think equivalent to that of the head of a nation. . . . In every instance I, my wife and the appropriate State officials, depending upon the nature of the trip and its purpose, have been given as extensive briefings as we wanted by State Department officials. . . .

Georgia has a particular advantage over some states in that we have our own built-in State Department in the Coca-Cola Company. They provide me ahead of time with much more penetrating analyses of what the country is, what its problems are, who its leaders are, and when I arrive there, provide me with an introduction to the leaders of that country in every realm of life in which we have an interest."

—November 12, 1974, Georgia; speech to the Commission on Foreign Relations

LEFT OUT

(Talking about the voters he was seeking to reach in 1970, including some who would normally vote for George Wallace . . .)

"They are average working people. What they want is someone in the governor's office who understands their problems, who has worked with his hands, who knows what it means to be left out, who knows what it means to be fearful of the system of justice, to have cold chills go up and down their spine when a patrolman stops them, who never has had any voice, for instance, in the mechanism of the Democratic Party, even though they do have an intense interest in politics.

"Well, I'm going to give them these things because I believe in it. . . . It's kind of a populist approach and this is going to be the major thrust of our campaign.

"These people are for me. I've talked to them. I've wooed them. They don't ask me for any commitment that's racist in nature or that would discriminate against anybody. They want some rights."

—April, 1970, Plains, Ga.;
interview

ACCESS

"Each month we schedule a visitors' day during which anyone can come to see me personally without an appointment. On these regular and well-publicized occasions the governor's office is filled with those who have questions, requests, suggestions and criticisms. It is always a very instructive and helpful ordeal."

—August 12, 1974; column by
Carter in *The New York Times*

JUDGES

"I have refrained completely from making any judicial appointments on the basis of political support or other factors, and have chosen, in every instance, Superior Court judges, quite often State judges Appellate Court judges, on the basis of merit analysis by a highly competent, open, qualified group of distinguished Georgians. I'm proud of this."

—May 4, 1974, Athens, Ga.;
Georgia Law Day speech

COOK

"I was in the governor's mansion for two years, enjoying the services of a very fine cook, who was a prisoner—a woman. One day she came to me, after she got over her two years of timidity, and said, 'Governor, I would like to borrow $250 from you.'

"I said, 'I'm not sure that a lawyer would be worth that much.'

"She said, 'I don't want to hire a lawyer; I want to pay the judge.'

"I thought it was a ridiculous statement for her; I felt that she was ignorant. But I found out she wasn't. She had been sentenced by a superior court judge in the state, who still serves, to seven years or $750. She had raised, early in her prison career, $500. I didn't lend her the money but I had Bill Harper, my legal aide, look into it. He found the circumstances were true. She was quickly released."

—May 4, 1974, Athens, Ga.;
Georgia Law Day speech

38

GEORGIA BUSING

(In February, 1972, Carter urged the state legislature to seek an anti-busing amendment to the U.S. Constitution, but said he would support a one-day school boycott "as a last resort.")

"If the legislature does not act on this amendment, it will be all right for Georgia parents to hold their children out of school briefly. . . .

"The massive forced busing of students such as that now taking place in Richmond County is the most serious threat to education I can remember."

—February 16, 1972, Atlanta

"I was faced with a massive effort supported by many political figures in Georgia to mount an all-out boycott against our public school system because of the threat of busing in Augusta. As an alternative to the boycott, and in order to hold down racial tension in the state, I said that a better way to handle it was to let the legislature pass a simple, non-binding resolution calling on the Congress to address the issue through a constitutional amendment, rather than having all of our kids leave the schools all over Georgia. The impact of my statement would defuse racial tension, and I don't think it was designed to prey on the divisive and emotional and racist attitudes that did exist in a few of our people."

—March 14, 1976, Washington;
CBS's "Face the Nation"

"My action could be interpreted as supporting a constitutional amendment (against busing). . . .

39

"I have shifted away from even that moderate stand. . . .

"My option as governor (in 1972) was a total boycott with violence."

—February 25, 1976, Boston; press conference

PLANNING

"When I was elected governor five years ago, we set up what we called 'Goals for Georgia.' We had 51 hearings around the state, confirmed it with Georgia State University analysis, and wrote down, so that the people could understand exactly what we hoped to achieve in the state in every realm of human life: in mental health, physical health, alcoholism treatment, drug control, tax reform, welfare reform, also judicial reform, transportation—a year, two years, five years, sometimes 20 years in the future. We put cost figures on the first five years. And every budget that I submitted to the legislature was submitted in accordance with those plans."

—February 23, 1976, Boston; '76 Presidential Forum

CONSENT

"I had lunch this week with the members of the Judicial Selection Committee, and they were talking about a consent search warrant. I said I didn't know what a consent search warrant was. They said, 'Well, that's when two policemen go to a house. One of them goes to the front door and knocks on it, and the other one runs around to the back door and yells "come in." ' I have to admit that as governor, quite often I search for ways to bring about my own hopes; not quite so stringently testing the law as that, but with a similar motivation."

—May 4, 1974, Athens, Ga.;
Georgia Law Day speech

WALLACE'S SHOOTING

"No matter how hard they try to avoid it, public officials tend to become almost dehumanized in the eyes of most people.

"This is one reason, I think that an incident like the attack on Gov. Wallace is such a shock.

"When you are in politics, you are not a person anymore. You are a governor or a senator or a president.

"An attack like this brings home to everybody what they tend to forget—that a public official has a family and friends whom he cares about and who care about him just as much as anyone else in our society."

—May 17, 1972; from an article
by Carter in the *Atlanta
Constitution*

LESTER MADDOX

Lester Maddox represents "the essence of the Democratic Party. He has compassion for the ordinary man. I am proud to be on the ticket with him.

"Despite reports you have heard, there had never been any difference between us in the primary."

> —October 26, 1970, Columbus, Ga.; speech at a Maddox fundraising dinner

"I think anyone who knows Georgia politics would avow that he and I have been bitter and constant political enemies."

> —November 30, 1975, Washington; CBS's "Face the Nation"

McGOVERN'S DEFENSE CUTS

George McGovern's proposed cuts in the Defense budget would be "a radical departure" from America's 200-year-old desire "to be able to defend itself."

The cuts would also have "a devasting effect" on Georgia.

> —June 1, 1972, Atlanta

LOBBYISTS

"I see the lobbyists in the state Capitol filling the halls on occasions. Good people, competent people, the most pleasant, personable, extroverted citizens of Georgia. Those are the characteristics that are required for a lobbyist. They represent good folks. But I tell you that when a lobbyist goes to represent the Peanut Warehousemen's Association of the Southeast, which I belong to, which I helped to organize, they go there to represent the peanut warehouseman. They don't go there to represent the customers of the peanut ware-houseman."

—May 4, 1974, Athens, Ga.;
Georgia Law Day speech

HUMPHREY—WALLACE

(A ticket of Hubert Humphrey and George Wallace, in 1972, would be acceptable to Carter and . . .)
". . . would do well in the South."

—June 7, 1972, Houston;
interview

LT. CALLEY

(In 1971, why did you proclaim American fighting man's day, in opposition to the conviction of Lt. William Calley?)

"I don't think that was said in support of or in opposition to the conviction of Lt. Calley. As you know, the Calley conviction took place in Georgia; it was a very highly emotional thing. And rather than focusing the attention of Georgia people on the Calley case itself, I tried to hold down violence and to take the sharp edge off the Calley conviction, which was a very vivid issue in Georgia at that time, by saying let's think about all of our fighting men that did perform well. But I have never been a supporter of Calley, nor have I ever deplored his conviction, nor have I ever in any way supported what he did. I think it was abominable, what he did."

—November 30, 1975, Washington;
CBS's "Face the Nation"

PRIDE

"I would like to talk to you for a few moments about some of the practical aspects of being a governor who is still deeply concerned about the inadequacies of a system of which it is obvious that you're so patently proud."

—May 4, 1974, Athens, Ga.;
Georgia Law Day speech

4

Politics and Politicking

MY OPPONENTS

"I think it's obvious that my opponents, who are very fine people, have had an absence of success."

—March 25, 1976, Madison, Wisc.; interview

INTIMATE

"I'd like to form an intimate relationship with the people of this country. And when I'm president, the country will be ours again."

—March 10, 1976, Springfield, Ill.; fundraising reception

MORE INTIMATE

"I want to have the kind of relationship with you as key and strong supporters on a personal plane. . . . I'd like you to feel toward me the same way I feel toward you. I feel close to you. I want you to be part of my family. When I get in the White House, I want to stay close to you."

—March 11, 1976, Chicago; fundraising dinner

COMBATIVE

"I'm going to run the kind of campaign that I don't think the othe rcandidates will want me to run with them (as a vice-presidential candidate). It will be tough, hard-hitting, combative . . . the kind I think the people want."

—January 21, 1975, Princeton, N.J.; interview

ANTI-WASHINGTON?

"I've never made an anti-Washington statement. . . ."

Government employees are mostly "good people" in a system that makes them "spend their time shuffling papers, smothered in red tape. . . .

"I know that it is possible for an irrational, ill-planned, inhuman system to grind down, discourage and virtually incapacitate the most dedicated and competent public servant."

—early May, 1976, Rockville, Md.; speech to rally

INSIDERS

"The people of this country know from bitter experience that we are not going to get these changes merely by shifting around the same group of insiders.

"The same old rhetoric, the same unkept promises and the same divisive appeals to one party faction, one section of the country, one race, religion, one interest group, are not enough. The insiders have had their chance and they have not delivered. And their time has run out.

"The time has come for the great Majority of Americans—those who have for too long been on the outside looking in—to have a president who will turn the government of this country inside out."

—February 17, 1976, Boston;
speech at rally

FUNDRAISING

"Do what you can to help us raise money. If you have friends and relatives who ca ngive us $5, $10, $100, ask them to do it quickly. . . .

"I've made 120 long distance calls in a day. You can too. Take a week off from work. You can call your friends and ask if they can send in $20, $50. It's just as much your country as it is mine."

—April 13, 1976, Atlanta;
rally

A STRANGER

(Why are you being criticized for failure to take positions?)

48

"The Washington political figure, including news-media persons" are upset "that someone unknown to them could be a success without their knowing it."

—March 11, 1976, Chicago; television interview

ENDORSEMENTS

"I have never asked for endorsements.
"My whole effort is to go directly to the people themselves. If groups endorse me—or don't endorse me—that's okay."

—December 9, 1975, Medford, Mass.; college address

(Carter, calling Sen. Birch Bayh on the telephone . . .)
"I need your help. I'd like for you to join in our campaign."

—April 27, 1976, according to Bayh

(Asked about his statement, the day after his private phone call to Bayh, that he had "never gone to anyone yet and asked them to endorse me. . . .")
"My point was that I have never depended on endorsements to put me in office."
The request to Bayh was "for his support and confidence—we did not talk about endorsement at that time."

—May 3, 1976, Fort Wayne; press conference

NO FACADE

"I believe the physical and mental strain of a tough campaign has an important role in our political system. The pressure and fatigue tend to strip away even the most carefully constructed facade and reveal basic strengths and flaws of character."

—September 5, 1975; column by
Carter in *The New York Times*

STOP CARTER

"My critics don't want to stop Carter. They want to stop the reforms I am committed to. They want to stop the people of this country from regaining control of their government. They want to preserve the status quo, to preserve politics as usual, to maintain at all costs their own entrenched, unresponsive, bankrupt, irresponsible political power.

"They know I do not believe in business as usual or politics as usual or a blind acceptance of the status quo."

—May 27, 1976, Cincinnati;
speech to AFL-CIO convention

MO'S ADS

"The advertisements being put on the air by Congressman Udall represent a breakdown in the relationships between the candidates that existed before. I deplore it very deeply."

—late May, 1976, Steubenville,
Ohio

BLACK SUPPORT

"If I've got one solid base of support around this country, it would be among the black people who know me."

—February 21, 1976, Roxbury, Mass.; headquarters opening

30 PRIMARIES

"I have never minded running in 30 primaries. If the primaries are an obstacle course, they are a necessary and wise one, for they are a test of all the qualities our people demand of their president.

"Our people ask that a president be both tough and gentle, both statesman and politician, both dreamer and fighter. You expect him to have the drive and stamina to reach the White House, and the wisdom and patience to govern wisely there."

—May 28, 1976, Ohio

HORSE-TRADING

(Asked if he would horse-trade for uncommitted delegates, if he needed them, at the National Convention . . .)

"It would depend on whether it was legitimate or profitable and if the terms of the agreement could be made public."

—May 25, 1976, New York

PICKING VICE PRESIDENTS

"There is no way to guarantee that a mistake won't be made. There's always the potential no matter how long you take to consider the vice president. I point out the Agnew affair, even more devastating than the Eagleton affair. And Nixon had a long time to consider him. He had worked with him for four years as vice president and still made a very serious mistake.

"But I'm a very careful and methodical man, and by the time I made a recommendation to the convention I would have considered three factors: first, who would be the person best qualified to lead the country if something should happen to me; second, someone who is basically compatible with me in political philosophy and stands on the major issues, who could support my programs and would be naturally inclined to keep the promises I have made during my campaign; and third, a consideration quite remote in importance, someone who would bring geographical or other balance to the ticket."

—January, 1976; interview

VERSUS FORD

"If President Ford runs, I think (the issue) would be an assessment of whether or not he is a leader. I think that President Ford is a good, honest, decent person. I know him well and have known him long before he became president. His wife has visited in our home, and I have been with him often. I think he is a very weak leader. I don't think that he shows any boldness or aggressiveness. I think he is a typical product of a lifetime in the Congress where everything is handled incrementally and through compromise. He has been quite timid in making his mind up about major substantive issues. There is no purpose presently to the government."

—April 11, 1975, Little Rock;
press conference

OTHER CANDIDATES

"They think I'm a snake oil salesman. They can't understand my appeal among so many different groups. They think, 'Well, if he's doing so great it's because he's saying different things to different people.' "

—May, 1976; airborne interview

AN EARLY ASSESSMENT

"I think personally that Jackson has already peaked, but that may be an underestimation of his strength. . . .

"Bentsen is probably in the race to stay. Udall in my judgment is still trying to decide whether or not to run. I think that, to be perfectly frank, Fred Harris and Gene McCarthy are just kind of fringe candidates."

—April 11, 1975, Little Rock;
press conference

JACKSON AND McGOVERN

(Asked about his support of Henry Jackson for president in 1972, and his opposition to George McGovern that year . . .)

"I think any human being changes with changing circumstances, but I haven't changed my basic concept. I did oppose George McGovern when he was running for the nomination. I supported George McGovern openly and very well after he got the Democratic nomination. I nominated Scoop Jackson in 1972 because I had known Scoop for 25 years. He came down to Atlanta and asked me to give the nominating speech. That was my first convention. I nominated him and I was very proud of the opportunity. Scoop is a good man and I certainly wouldn't say anything against him. I intend to defeat him in the primaries. . . .

"I am not as hawkish as Sen. Jackson on some aspects of foreign policy. I am certainly not as liberal on many elements of importance to the American people as was George McGovern.

"I would put myself, in my opinion, above either one of them as a candidate for president."

—December 15, 1974, Washington; NBC's "Meet the Press"

HENRY JACKSON

"I think Jackson has severed several relationships with his very strong supporters without picking up any new supporters. There's a constant shift of posture. . . . He had the support of the ultra-hawks, but now he has shaken their support off and hasn't picked up any new support. I think his constant excessive concentration on the Israeli question not only embarassed some of the Jewish leaders in our nation, but also indicated he was doing this for political gain."

—August, 1975, Plains, Ga.; interview

ANSWERING JACKSON

(On the day Henry Jackson had accused him of shifting positions . . .)
"I think Sen. Jackson is one of the finest men I've ever met. I look forward to working with him when I'm president."

—February 17, 1976, Boston; rally

BETWEEN FRIENDS

"I want to make it clear to the audience that the argument here is between two friends. There's nobody in the Congress that I think more of then I do Sen. Jackson. He's been in the Congress 35 years; he knows what he's talking about, except every now and then. . . .

"Every now and then, in addition to sharing all the good things the Congress has done, he's got to bear some of the responsibility for the bad things that Congress has done."

—March 1, 1976, Miami; '76 Presidential Forum

JERRY BROWN

". . . is a fine young man" but "a vote cast for him is a vote cast away from you to the political machines seeking a deadlocked convention."

—early May, 1976, Rockville, Md.

BIRCH BAYH

"Three or four months ago, Birch Bayh could have been a very formidable opponent. He first let it be known that he was going to announce in May. Then he sent word it would be in June. I saw Bayh out in California last weekend and he said he might announce this weekend. I think the longer he delays the less his political possibilities are. But I think he would be very attractive candidate."

—August, 1975, Plains, Ga.;
interview

LLOYD BENTSEN

"I don't think Bentsen likes to work. He goes to a few very small receptions that are held for very wealthy people, most of whom are Republicans. And he will very quietly slip out of the community without making any sort of effort to reach the political consciousness of the community."

—August, 1975, Plains, Ga.;
interview

MORRIS UDALL

"He's a better candidate than the others I have mentioned (Jackson, Bentsen and Bayh). He has concentrated his efforts substantially in New Hampshire and in Wisconsin. I think that because of this his campaign in the rest of the nation has suffered to some degree. He has had a problem with his health. He has missed three or four engagements because he became nauseated or because he had a backache."

—August, 1975, Plains, Ga.;
interview

FRED HARRIS

"Harris is my favorite among my opponents."

—April 25, 1976, Pittsburgh;
dinner with staff

TED KENNEDY

(After being told that Kennedy had called Carter "indefinite and imprecise" on some issues . . .)

"I'm glad I don't have to depend on Kennedy or Hubert Humphrey, or anyone like that, to put me in office.

"I don't have to kiss his ass."

—May 18, 1976, Newark, N.J.;
talking with staff

GEORGE WALLACE

". . . will probably be running for president in 1988, if he's able."

—late 1975, Naples, Fla.;
press conference

"He raises a lot of money and spends very little."

—late 1975, Naples, Fla.;
press conference

PAST SOUTHERN CANDIDATES

". . . were more interested in sending a message to Washington than in getting elected."

—January, 1975, Sacramento;
interview

SEN. ADLAI STEVENSON

"Some of the senators say he's not very bright."

—April 25, 1976, Pittsburgh;
dinner with staff

MAYNARD JACKSON

(After being told by a staffer that Atlanta Mayor Maynard Jackson would endorse him in return for some political help . . .)
"Jackson can kiss my ass and you tell him that. I'm through calling him."

—April 19, 1976, Atlanta; staff
meeting

FORD OR REAGAN?

(Would you rather run against Gerald Ford or Ronald Reagan?)
"I can't think of any preference. I thought about it a lot and the general wisdom is that Ford would be the more formidable opponent. I don't see it that way. I think it'll be a toss-up, and when I just sort of let myself analyze it subjectively, I can't detect within my thinking any real preference of running against Ford or not."

—June 14, 1976, airborne interview

GERALD FORD

"I think Ford is a non-leader. He has not taken any comprehensive approach to the basic problems of this country except in the case of energy. In that instance he has just adopted the oil companies' policy and that is to raise the price of oil higher and higher and let the oil companies reap greater and greater profits."

—August, 1975, Plains, Ga.; interview

BLAME IT ON . . .

"Anything you don't like about Washington, you can blame it on President Ford."

—early May, 1976, Texas

5

Politics and Politicians

AGGRESSIVE

"Most of my attitude toward government is very aggressive. I wouldn't be a quiescent or a timid president."

—April 29, 1976; airborne interview

ONLY HUMAN

"I never had seen a president before I was elected governor except Harry Truman when we laid the keel of the USS Nautilus in 1952, the first atomic submarine, in New London. I was a lieutenant working for Admiral Rickover. I saw him at a distance. And to me the presidency was always a very exalted and very revered office. It still is. And then, after I got to be elected governor, I began to meet people who were either president or who expected to be president. Richard Nixon, Agnew, McGovern, Wallace, Reagan, Rockefeller, Muskie; and I didn't feel inferior anymore. I feel that I am as qualified to be president as any one of them."

—April 11, 1975, Little Rock;
press conference

FDR

"I think the thing about Franklin D. Roosevelt that people remember most is that he understood people and he stayed close to them. He told them what was going on and he analyzed their problems frankly, and he never did mislead anyone."

—August 14, 1973, Warm Springs, Georgia;
speech to members of the Warm Springs Foundation

MAYOR RICHARD DALEY

. . . is a "miracle man. . . .
"I have learned a lot from Mayor Daley. I saw in 1972 how the party was split when the Illinois delegation was not seated."

—July 3, 1976, Chicago;
fundraising reception with Daley

EARL BUTZ

"One of the reasons I work as a campaigner six days a week from six in the morning to eleven at night is so that when I get in the White House I can send Earl Butz back where he came from."

—March 10, 1976,
Marion, Ill.; at a rally

KENNEDY AND JOHNSON

"Kennedy and Johnson, in my opinion, didn't do enough to bring blacks to the policymaking positions in the government. I think Johnson had a much greater feel for it than Kennedy did. Kennedy was not one of them—he didn't understand their special needs."

—June 14, 1976, airborne interview

LYNDON JOHNSON

"Lyndon Johnson was never accepted by the liberal Eastern establishment. He did things that had been talked about for generations, in the field of social progress and alleviating discrimination—Voting Rights Act, Civil Rights Acts. For some reason he was never quite accepted. I don't know why. . . ."

(Why do you think you can be accepted by the Eastern liberal establishment?)

"I'm sure of myself. I'm not sure that Johnson was ever sure of himself when he was president. I don't feel ill-at-ease when I'm in a Harvard professor's house and there's two or three hundred people around asking questions."

(Do you ever play a role?)
"I'm sure I do."

> —June 14, 1976, airborne
> interview

McGOVERN, 1972

"We wound up with a very poor candidate, who is I think a good man but a terrible candidate, George McGovern."

> —April 11, 1975, Little Rock;
> press conference

NIXON, 1968

"We lost the election that year (1968) to men who governed without love and without laughter, to men who promised law and order and gave us crime and oppression."

> —June 1, 1976, Los Angeles;
> speech at the Martin Luther
> King Hospital

NIXON-VIETNAM

"I believe that President Nixon is doing all that he possibly can to bring the war to an end.

"I have a very keen interest in the war in Vietnam. My oldest son is in Vietnam and we have not heard from him in three weeks. I can think of nothing that I would rather see at this moment than an end to the war."

—October 17, 1969, Savannah; speech to a civic club

WHY THEY'RE VOTING

"In 1968, in 1972, there was a strong division among the supporters of different candidates depending upon the positions they took on issues—for or against the war, for or against abortion, for or against amnesty, for or against gun control. That's not the case this year. The people have been hurt so deeply in this country with Vietnam, Cambodia, Watergate, CIA, that they're looking for somebody they can trust. . . . They might have very deep concerns about an issue, but that's not why they're voting."

—late April, 1976; interview

THOMAS JEFFERSON

"I've read parts of the embarrassing (Watergate) transcripts, and I've seen the proud statement of a former attorney general, who protected his boss, and now brags on the fact that he tiptoed through a minefield and came out 'clean.' I can't imagine somebody like Thomas Jefferson tiptoeing through a minefield on the technicalities of the law, and then bragging about being clean afterwards.

"I think our people demand more than that. I believe that everyone in this room is in a position of responsibility as a preserver of the law in its purest form ought to remember the oath that Thomas Jefferson and others took when they practically signed their own death warrant, writing the Declaration of Independence—to preserve justice and equity and freedom and fairness, they pledged their lives, their fortunes and their sacred honor."

—May 4, 1974, Athens, Ga.;
Georgia Law Day speech

WATERGATE

"I think the American people understand Watergate; I think they're sick of it. I think they've been embarrassed by it. They can make their own judgments about whether or not Ford and Nixon had a previous agreement concerning the pardon. I take Ford at his word that there was no secret agreement.

"For me to raise that question would be a divisive thing. I think it's an emotional issue and I don't think it would be a reason for me to accrue political advantage and I don't think it would be healthy for the country. So I don't intend to raise the Watergate issue."

—March 25, 1976, Madson, Wisc.;
interview

THE DUTY OF POLITICS

"One of the things that (Reinhold) Niebuhr says is that the sad duty of the political system is to establish justice in a sinful world."

—May 4, 1974, Athens, Ga.;
Georgia Law Day speech

REFLECTION

"Insofar as my political campaign has been successful it is because I have learned from our people, and have accurately reflected their concerns, their frustrations and their desires."

—June 23, 1976, New York; speech to the Foreign Policy Association

MORE PERFECT UNION

"I was at the Liberty Bell in Philadelphia the day before the Pennsylvania people voted and I thought back to what our country was 200 years ago. We have a tendency to think it was perfect. It wasn't. It wasn't.

"George Washington had slaves. Thomas Jefferson had slaves. It took almost 100 years to make changes. Then it took women a long time to get a chance to vote and young people a long time to get a chance to vote. Yet they could fight and die for our country.

"So our country is almost 200 years old and it's still a young country. It's still growing, it's still searching, it still has a long way to go. We got life, we got liberty. We still got more liberty to get and we still got a lot of happiness to find."

—April, 1976, Indianapolis; speech in a black church

WHY

"The American people are competent. Why shouldn't the government be competent? The people tell the truth. Why should our government lie?"

—March 10, 1976, Champaign, Ill.; addressing students

VISION

"I have tried, for 16 months, in thousands of talks across America, to express my vision of this nation's future. It is a vision that has grown and ripened as I have traveled and talked and gotten to know our people better.

"Mine is a vision of an America that is, in Bob Dylan's phrase, busy being born, not busy dying.

"I see an America poised not only at the brink of a new century, but at the dawn of a new era of honest, compassionate, responsive government.

"I see an America that has turned away from scandals and corruption and official cynicism and finally become a government as decent as her people.

"I see an America with a tax system that does not cheat the average wage earner.

"I see an America with a job for every man and woman who can work, and a decent standard of living for those who cannot.

"I see an America that knows no higher priority, no greater mission, than excellence in the education of our children.

"I see an American foreign policy that is firm and consistent and generous, and that can once again be a beacon for the hopes of the world.

"I see an America on the move again, united, its wounds healed, its head high, an America with pride in its past and faith in its future, a diverse and vital nation, moving into its third century with confidence and competence and compassion, an America that lives up to the majesty of its Constitution and the simple decency of its people.

"I see an American president who does not govern by vetoes and negativism, but with vigor and vision and affirmative leadership, a president who is not isolated from our people but feels their pain and shares their dreams and takes his strength from you."

—May 28, 1976, Ohio

BEFORE I GO OUT

"There's no doubt in my mind that before I go out of office the budget will be balanced and we will have zero-base budgeting and the government reorganization will be proper and we'll have a sunshine law (requiring open meetings), and that the harmony between the White House and the Congress will be restored. It might be very contentious, might be very competitive and it might even be combative, but I think the Congress is eager to see cooperation now."

—June 14, 1976; airborne interview

OUR GOVERNMENT

"Nowhere in the Constitution of our country, nor the Bill of Rights, nor the Declaration of Independence, the Emancipation Proclamation, nor the Old Testament or the New Testament do you find the words 'economy' or 'efficiency.'

"You find other words that are much more important—words like 'fairness,' 'equity.' Words like 'decency' and 'honesty.' Words like 'commitment' and 'self-reliance' and 'patriotism.' Words like 'brotherhood' and 'compassion' and 'love' and a lot of other words that describe what a person, individually, ought to be, and which also describe exactly what the government of that person ought to be.

"We ought not to lower our standards in the government. Our government in Washington ought to be an inspiration to us all, and not a source of shame."

—April 16, 1975, Misenheimer, N.C.; speech to college students

LEADERSHIP

"The Congress, or the legislative branch of government, is inherently incapable of leadership. Our Founding Fathers never thought that Congress would lead this nation. There's only one place that leadership can be derived, and that's in the White House. And in the absence of that leadership in planning, reorganization and major structural changes, there won't be any leadership."

—February 23, 1976, Boston; '76 Presidential Forum

BRITISH

"Last year I was in England as a guest of the British government. I attended the House of Commons, and I sat there fascinated watching the tough, penetrating cross-examination of a cabinet member who is responsible for education by the members of the House of Commons. . . . Estes Kefauver proposed that cabinet members in this country present themselves to Congress, preferably in a joint session, and let written questions be submitted ahead of time and then let open questions from the floor be asked. . . .

"It ought to be done and, if I'm elected, it will be

done, if the Congress will accept the offer, and I will also request that those sessions be televised."

—April 16, 1975, Misenheimer, N.C.; speech to college students

PERSONAL FINANCES

"Complete revelation of all business and financial involvements of all major officials should be required and none should be continued which constitute a possible conflict with the public interest. I have released an audit of my personal finances and will do so annually throughout my term of office. I will insist that the same requirement apply to the vice president and to those appointed to major policymaking positions in my administration. As president, I will seek legislation to make such disclosure mandatory."

—January 26, 1976; position paper

"There are a lot of darn good people in this country who say correctly, 'I don't want my private business affairs to be revealed to the public.' In my judgment, they ought not to serve in public office. Let them find some other place to serve."

—April 16, 1975; Misenheimer, N.C.; speech to college students

GIFTS

"I don't see any reason for any public official to receive any gift of value. . . . There is no reason for a president or a governor or a congressman or a senator to take a gift from anybody. If it is a small personal gift, it ought to be revealed, to let the folks back home look it over and say if it's personal or not."

—April 16, 1975, Misenheimer,
N.C.; speech to college
students

LOCKED DOORS

"The whole government's enshrouded in secrecy. I'm a strong, fervent, deeply-committed, loyal Democrat. But I see no reason why a Democratically-controlled Ways and Means Committee should pass a tax measure behind locked doors. I see no reason why a Democratically-controlled Appropriations Committee should spend my tax money with the doors locked. It ought to be opened, because every lobbyist in Washington knows what went on behind those locked doors, but I was governor of five million people and I didn't know."

—February 23, 1976, Boston;
'76 Presidential Forum

PRESS CONFERENCES

"During the campaign and as president, I will make myself available to the news media. Press conferences will be held monthly or more often throughout my administration."

—January 26, 1976; position paper

CAVEAT EMPTOR

"There was a time when the average person who works in a post office or filling station or who digs ditches or rides a truck or who grows peanuts didn't take much interest in politics as such. They let their voices be expressed for them by powerful people in the community, an editor or sheriff or judge or prominent lawyer or someone of that sort. But lately there has swept this country an attitude of what might be called consumerism. There's a great distrust on the part of the average citizen when he sees fancy advertisements or hears politicians bragging on the kinds of things they have done or are going to do. Many prominent businessmen are disconcerted because the public is no longer as gullible as it used to be."

—January 21, 1974, Georgia; address before The Georgia Municipal Association

6

God's Will . . .

GOD'S WILL

"I pray frequently—not continually, but many times a day. When I have a sense of peace, and self assurance—I don't know where it comes from—what I'm doing is a right thing. I assume, maybe in an unwarranted way, that that's doing God's will."

—May 6, 1976; television interview

A GREAT CHRISTIAN

"I thought I was really a great Christian. And one day the preacher gave this sermon. I don't remember a thing he said. I just remember the title . . . 'If You were Arrested For Being A Christian, Would There Be Any Evidence To Convict You?'

"And my answer by the time the sermon was over was 'No.' I never had really committed myself totally to God. My Christian beliefs were superficial. They were based primarily on pride. I never had done much for other people. I was always thinking about myself. And I changed somewhat for the better. I formed a much more intimate relationship with Christ."

—May 6, 1976, television
interview

THE LAW

"I'm a Sunday School teacher, and I've always known that the structure of law is founded on the Christian ethic that you shall love the Lord your God and your neighbor as yourself—a very high and perfect standard."

—May 4, 1974, Athens, Ga.;
Georgia Law Day speech

GOLDEN RULE

"If we insist that the golden rule be applied in all public matters, then potential inequities can be prevented, and wrongs can be righted."

—1975; from Carter's autobiography,
Why Not the Best?

SECOND COMING

"We should live our lives as though Christ were coming this afternoon.

"Suppose you were informed that Jesus was going to come tonight and you had just five hours to live. What would you do to get ready for Christ's presence?

"You might think of all the people you had hurt, or of those for whom you had some hatred in your heart, and you might get on the phone and call them and say: 'Look, I'm sorry.'

"You might talk to your wife about something you had said to her or had done, or to someone you had intended to talk to about Christ.

"Those things we would do in those five hours are the things we should be doing this afternoon. Jesus hasn't told us when he's coming, but we should be ready."

> —March, 1976, Plains, Ga.;
> speech to Baptist Bible class

EXALTING OURSELVES

"We have a tendency to exalt ourselves and to dwell on the weaknesses and mistakes of others. I have come to realize that in every person there is something fine and pure and noble, along with a desire for self-fulfillment."

> —1975; from Carter's autobiography,
> *Why Not the Best?*

SACRIFICE

(In 1967, Carter was upset over losing his race for governor, and talked to his sister, evangelist Ruth Carter Stapleton.)

"Ruth asked me if I would give up anything for Christ, if I would give up my life and my possessions—everything. I said I would. Then she asked me if I would be willing to give up politics. I thought for a long time and had to admit that I would not."

—April, 1976; interview

BORN AGAIN

"I was quoted as saying I was 'twice born,' but the expression I use is 'born again.' We believe that the first time we're born as children, it's human life given to us; and when we accept Jesus as our Saviour it's a new life. That's what 'born again' means. I was baptized when I was eleven years old. I never did have a personal feeling of intimacy with Christ until, I'd say, ten, twelve years ago, and then I began to see much more clearly the significance of Christ in my life, and it changed my attitudes dramatically."

(How?)

"I became much more deeply committed to study and using my example to explain to other people about Christ. I did a lot of missionary work."

(How might your religious beliefs guide your political career?)

"It has no particular political significance. It's something that's with me every day."

—March 16, 1976, Washington; interview

CHRISTIAN PRIDE

"In my lay witness efforts I have learned about the almost insurmountable obstacle of 'Christian pride.' An obvious belief that I am good and that I am holy often prevents the feeling of concern, compassion and love toward those who are assessing their needs for Christ."

—June 13, 1974, Dallas, Texas; address
before the Southern Baptist Convention

PAUL TILLICH

"One of my favorite philosophers or theologians is Paul Tillich, who, when he defined religion said, 'Religion is a search for the truth about man's existence and his relationship to God,' and goes on in a fairly comprehensive treatise to say that when a man loses the inclination to search for a closer relationship with God and his fellowmen and rests on his own laurels and his own achievements, at that point, to a major degree, he loses his religion."

—August 7, 1973, Athens, Ga.; speech to
the Georgia Association of Colleges

RIVER JORDAN

"I spent a good deal of time traveling in the nation of Israel. . . . I went to Bethlehem where Christ was born. I went to Nazareth. . . .

I walked around the shores of the Sea of Galilee. I went down to Jordan's river and I swam in the Dead Sea. It made a great impression on me. But the main thing that I saw there was the simplicity of Jesus' life. Little mules and a lot of chinaberry trees—it made me feel at home—a lot of doves and the land isn't very rich. The Jordan River is about half as wide as this church. I always thought it was a big river about the size of the Mississippi. But the point I make to you is the simplicity of Christ's life."

> —April, 1976, Indianapolis; speech in a black church

THE DOUBLE STANDARD

"The standards of government should exemplify the highest attributes of mankind, and not the lowest common denominator. There is no legitimate reason for different standards in our home, our office, our church, or our government. In every component of life we should continually strive for perfection as commanded by God."

> —June 13, 1974, Dallas, Texas; address before the Southern Baptist Convention

QUESTIONING THE BIBLE

"I find it difficult to question Holy Scripture, but I admit that I do have trouble with Paul sometimes, especially when he says that a woman's place is with her husband, and that she should keep quiet and cover her head in church. I just can't go along with him on that."

—April, 1976; interview

CIVIL DISOBEDIENCE

"The lesson this morning taught very clearly that a Christian's duty . . . is to obey the civil authorities." A distinction should be drawn "when a public servant . . . disobeys the word of God."

"At that point, it's the responsibility of a Christian to ask whether his government accurately reflects the will of God . . . and if the judgment is that it doesn't obey the will of God, then the duty of the Christian is to obey the will of God."

(What should civil authorities do when a person declares he cannot obey a law because of his religious beliefs?)

"The Bible teaches in that case that the citizen has to suffer the consequences of the law."

"We are supposed to have a responsibility as citizens to make sure that the law, the government, the public authorities do provide for honesty, for concern, for equality of opportunity, for love.

"So we have a responsibility to try to shape the government so that it does exemplify the teachings of God; to obey the government and—if at times the government, because of an inadequate influence of ourselves, violates, in our opinion, the rule of God—that we're supposed to accept the punishment administered to us by the state."

—June 27, 1976, Plains, Ga.; news conference after going to men's Sunday school class

REQUEST

"I don't pray to God to let me win an election, I pray to ask God to let me do the right thing."

—April, 1976; interview

7

...And Jimmy's

JIMMY'S WILL

(Spoken to his sister, Ruth Carter Stapleton, who was complaining of campaign exhaustion.)

"Honey, I can will myself to sleep until 10:30 a.m. and get my ass beat, or I can will myself to get up at 6 a.m. and become president."

—March, 1976; recounted by
Ruth Stapleton

TESTING

Disciplinary punishment for plebes at Annapolis ". . . was sometimes a brutal form of training and testing. If one ever showed any weakness, he was assaulted from all sides with punishment and harassment, and forced out of the academy."

> —1975, from Carter's autobiography, *Why Not the Best?*

COURTLINESS

"Sometimes people misjudge mine and your courtliness—I hope that I maintain it most of the time—(for) weakness or intimations of assuaging other people's needs or feelings."

> —May 2, 1976; airborne interview

QUIET

"I'm a very quiet person. But I don't let anybody push me around."

> —February 27, 1976; Boston interview

ACCOMODATION

"There are some groups with whom I feel perfectly at home, and some I don't. But in general I'm able to accomodate different kinds of groups fairly well. And that's one of the things I've always tried to do in the speech—to figure out in my own mind the compatibilities between me and them. But I'm not always successful."

> —June 14, 1976; airborne interview

PRIVATE PROPERTY

"I don't belong to anybody."

—March 10, 1976, Champaign,
Ill.; addressing students

COMPROMISE

"I was never much able to fit into a back room and compromise things away I believe in. And that's a very legitimate source of criticism for me. I'm not a good compromiser."

—May 6, 1976; television
interview

HYMAN RICKOVER

"During my last two years in the Navy I worked for a remarkable man by the name of Rickover. He is probably the greatest engineer this nation ever produced. He is a great scientist and is completely dedicated. He works very, very hard. He will be 75 years old this year.

"In years gone by he has been responsible for all the nuclear power generation for the Navy atomic submarines and the Atomic Energy Commission. Further, he has absolutely no tact—doesn't care for anything. As a matter of fact, all the time I worked for him he never said a decent word to me.

"However, he did change my life because he had one characteristic, and still has it, which has always been unique. He would never accept mediocrity or low average achievement in relation to anything he did or anyone under him did.

"I helped him and a few others develop the first two atomic submarines and I worked at the General Electric Company at that time and whenever the admiral would come around to inspect my work, if I had done a perfect job—which wasn't too often, but every now and then I did—he never said a word, never once did he say, 'good job, Jimmy' or 'well done, Carter.' If he found no fault, he simply looked, turned around and walked away.

"However, if I made the slightest mistake, in one of the loudest and most obnoxious voices I ever heard, he would turn around and tell the other people in the area what a horrible disgrace I was to the Navy and that I ought to be back in the oldest and slowest and smallest submarine from which I had come."

—March 15, 1975, Pittsburgh;
speech to the National
Wildlife Federation

THE INTERVIEW

"I remember the first time I met the Admiral (Rickover). We were in a room almost a quarter as large as this one. There was one table in the room and a chair on each side. I was being interviewed for a job and that interview lasted three and a half hours.

"He looked right between my eyes the whole time. He never smiled. He let me choose any subject I wanted to talk about and, of course, I carefully chose a subject about which I knew the most at the time—navigation, seamanship, foreign affairs, music, art, drama, whatever it was—and then with questions of increasing difficulty in each instance he proved that I did not know anything about the subject I had chosen.

"Toward the end of our interview I was sitting there in a cold sweat and he asked me a question in relation to which I could finally redeem myself.

"He asked, 'How did you stand in your class at Annapolis?'

"Well, I had done very well and so my chest swelled up with pride and I replied, 'Sir, I stood so-and-so- in a class of 765.' (Elsewhere Carter says it was 59th in a class of 820.)

"Well, I sat back to wait for a favorable reaction and the congratulations never came. I found out later, for example, he had stood number one in his class.

"He then asked me another question. He said, 'Did you do your best?'

"I started to say 'yes' but then I remembered for a part of the time when I was there there were times when I could have learned a little bit more about things, weapons, seamanship, navigation and so I gulped a couple of times and I said, 'No sir, I did not always do my best.'

"Well, he sat there for a long time looking at me and then he turned his chair around to end the interview and asked me one final question, somethiing which I have never been able to forget and to which I have never been able to think of a good answer to.

"He asked 'Why not?'

"Well, after a while I got up and walked out of the room."

> —March 15, 1975, Pittsburgh;
> speech to the national
> Wildlife Federation

TURTLE

"I don't know how to compromise on any principle I believe is right. Georgia Secretary of State Ben Fort-

son . . . once called me 'as stubborn as a South
Georgia turtle.' "

—1975; from Carter's autobiography, *Why Not the Best?*

DEDICATION OF LIFE

"As a scientist, I was working constantly, along
with everyone who professes that dedication of life, to
probe, probe every day of my life for constant change
for the better. It's completely anachronistic in the
make-up of a nuclear physicist or an engineer or a
scientist to be satisfied with what we've got, or to rest
on the laurels of past accomplishments. It's the nature
of the profession.

"As a farmer, the same motivation persists. Every
farmer I know of, who is worth his salt or who's just
average, is ahead of the experiment stations and the
research agronomist in finding better ways, changing
ways to plant, cultivate, utilize herbicides, gather, cure,
sell farm products. The competition for innovation is
tremendous, equivalent to the realm of nuclear physics
even.

"In my opinion, it's different in the case of lawyers.
And maybe this is a circumstance that is so inhererently
true that it can't be changed."

—May 4, 1974, Athens, Ga.;
Georgia Law Day speech

FLYING SAUCERS

"I don't laugh at people any more when they say
they've seen UFOs, because I've seen one myself. . . .

"One night I was getting ready to speak to a Lion's

Club in southwest Georgia (in 1973) and 20 or so members and myself were standing outside when there was a light in the western sky that got brighter and brighter and then disappeared. . . .

"I think it was the light beckoning me to enter the California primary."

—May 11, 1975, Washington; press conference

PREACHING

"I didn't come here to tell you how to run your business. I didn't come here to preach to you. I didn't come here to decide what is right and wrong or to make any sort of pontifications like that.

"I have to admit that I have had a tendency, and I have had it for a long time."

—April 16, 1975, Misenheimer, N.C.; speech to college students

CAUTIOUS

"I'm always very cautious about what I say."

—February 21, 1976, Worcester, Mass.; interview

IN PRIVATE

(Asked if he had said privately that Defense spending might have to be increased . . .)

"I'm not a liar. I don't make a statement in private contrary to what I make in public."

—May 2, 1976, Terre Haute, Ind.; press conference

INSINUATION

"Ordinarily I'm quite easygoing and don't like to argue. When somebody insinuates that I'm a liar, I resent it. I think that's a natural human reaction."

—May 2, 1976; airborne interview

POLITICAL SUICIDE

"If there is ever evidence that I have changed my position from one place to another it would be suicidal because ever since early in January I have had the constant attention of the national news media . . . and if there was ever any evidence put forward that I took a different position in one part of the country to another or from one month to another, it would be political suicide and I don't intend to commit that suicide and don't have any inclination to equivocate or mislead anybody."

—late April, 1976; interview

NEED

"I need you, all of you. I need your advice, your criticism, your intimacy. My strength, my support, my ability, comes out of people like you. I want you to

ĸnow when I'm in the White House you'll have a
friend there. You can come and see me, tell me your
troubles. . . .

"If I ever tell a lie, if I ever mislead you, if I ever
betray a trust or a confidence I want you to come and
take me out of the White House."

—March, 1976, Florida; speech

QUIT?

(If someone produced evidence that you had lied in
this campaign, would you quit?)
"I think I would, because I haven't told a lie."

—May 6, 1976; television
interview

AUTO RACING

"I have always been fascinated with auto racing too.
I used to go to Daytona Beach, Fla., for just about
every race down there. . . .

"Alf and Madelyn Knight (superintendent of the
Atlanta International Speedway and his wife) and I
go back a long way. We've been friends for years and
years.

"Back in the old days, Alf would get tickets for me
and my family. Never would let me pay for them.

"So I'd always get the biggest paper sack around.
Then I'd fill it just as full of peanuts as I could."

—February, 1971, Atlanta

REINHOLD NIEBUHR AND BOB DYLAN

"I read a lot and listen a lot. One of the sources for my understanding about the proper application of justice and the system of equity is from reading Reinhold Niebuhr, one of his books. . . . The other source of my understanding about what's right and wrong in this society is from a friend of mine, a poet named Bob Dylan. After listening to his records about 'The Ballad of Hattie Carol' and 'Like a Rolling Stone' and 'The Times, They Are A-Changing,' I've learned to appreciate the dynamism of change in a modern society."

—May 4, 1974, Athens, Ga.;
Georgia Law Day speech

BOOKS

"As far as books that I think have made a good impression on me, I think my favorite book of all time, strangely enough, is *Let Us Now Praise Famous Men* by James Agee, because of the analysis of the way I lived. That was the way I grew up. As far as an analysis of the presidents are concerned, *Presidential Character* (by James David Barber) is the best book I've ever read."

—March 25, 1976, Madison, Wisc.;
interview

POETRY

"As far as poetry goes, I like a lot of poets, but my favorite is Dylan Thomas. For years, my three children and my wife and I would sit down at night with recordings of Dylan Thomas himself reciting his poems

95

and we would analyze one poem a week, and try to
see what every word in his poems meant. He's by far
my favorite."

—March 25, 1976, Madison, Wisc.;
interview

POP

"In present music, I think, strangely enough, my
affinity for music has shifted from classical music to
a much more contemporary music. Bob Dylan is a
good friend of mine. I like Paul Simon. I like the
Marshall Tucker Band. I like Greg Allman and the
Allman Brothers. They're my friends. They raise money
for me. I look toward them almost as though they
were my own children."

—March 25, 1976, Madison, Wisc.;
interview

CLASSICAL

"All my education has been in technical schools,
but all through that period I expanded my mind by
studying. When I was in the Naval Academy, I spent
most of my free time with classical music. We got
paid $4 a month the first year, $7 a month the second
year. I spent all my money on classical records. We
would buy two or three versions, for instance, of a
Wagner aria or a Rachmaninoff concerto and we
would compare the techniques of the pianists or the
singers."

—March 25, 1976, Madison, Wisc.;
interview

PORNOGRAPHY

. . . is having "a devastating effect on our society."
"We need to educate the people who buy it. People who buy it need some sort of psychiatric help."

> —May 5, 1971, Atlanta; declaring
> "Fight Pornography Week"

KIDS' TV

"We've got the first amendment guaranteeing free speech, but it is ridiculous, in my opinion, to have the national networks show movies with filthy language in them, and suggestive sexual scenes, during the times of day when an eight-year-old is watching television.
"Basically it comes down to inducing people to strive for ethics and morality and excellence and goodness rather than appealing to the baser instincts of our people."

> —late January, 1976, New
> Hampshire; interview

TV NO

(What's your favorite television show?)
"I don't watch television."

> —March 25, 1976, Madison, Wisc.;
> interview

JOHNNY CARSON

Carter said he heard Johnny Carson do the answer-and-question bit on the Tonight Show.

"The answer was: '60 minutes.'

"And the question was: 'How long does it take Jimmy Carter to brush his teeth?'"

—June 30, 1976, Philadelphia; speech at a fundraiser

NO JOKE

"I'm not a very good joke teller."

—June 29, 1976; airborne interview

PRE-MARITAL AFFAIRS

Carter said a reporter, referring to Betty Ford's famous interview, asked him how he would feel if his daughter had a pre-marital affair.

"If told him that Mrs. Carter and I would be deeply hurt and shocked and disappointed . . . because our daughter is only seven years old."

—late 1975; Naples, Fla.; speech to Democrats

EXTRA-MARITAL AFFAIRS

"I think my wife . . . is sure of my loyalty. . . . She knows how hard I work. She knows how tired I am every night. She knows I have 50 or 60 reporters watching me day and night."

> —June 1, 1976; Long Beach, Calif.; answering a question at a senior citizens reception

EXTRA-MARITAL SEX

"I believe very deeply in the Bible and Christ taught us not to have extramarital sex."

> —February 22, 1976, Salem, N.H.; rally

THE MORAL THING

"Obviously the moral thing to do is to abstain from intercourse unless you are married."

> —January 21, 1976, Guilford, N.H.; speech to high school students

LEGISLATING MORALS

"If you should pass a law, as we did a number of years ago, that alcohol is illegal, that might be a moral step that would be approved by many people. But society just didn't accept it, and wouldn't accept it now. So when you go too far in trying to legislate morals, people react against it, and the law becomes ineffective."

(The fact that alcohol is legal and marijuana is illegal—is that a double standard?)

"There are those who think people ought to be able to do anything they want to themselves, as long as they don't hurt anybody else. I don't agree with that. I personally don't approve of the use of marijuana. I wish we didn't have any marijuana in the whole world. I wish we didn't have any heroin in the whole world."

(What about alcohol?)

"Well, that would suit me fine, too, if we didn't have alcohol. But there are certain things you can legislate and certain things you can't."

—late January, 1976, New Hampshire; interview

SHUCKS

(You drink?)
"Sometimes."
(You swear?)
"Sometimes."
(Think you'll swear if you finish fourth in Massachusetts?)
"Yes, I think I will."

—February 27, 1976, Boston; interview

AN ORDINARY MAN

"I have never claimed to be better or wiser than any other person. I think my greatest strength is that I am an ordinary man, just like all of you, one who has worked and learned and loved his family and made mistakes and tried to correct them without always succeeding."

—May 28, 1976, Ohio

BEST

"It is now time to stop and to ask ourselves the question which my last commanding officer, Admiral Hyman Rickover, asked me and every other young naval officer who serves or has served in an atomic submarine.

"For our nation—for all of us—that question is: 'Why not the best?' "

—December 12, 1974, Washington; announcement speech

8

Civil Rights

RACE

"I believe I know our people as well as anyone. Based on this knowledge of Georgians, north and south, rural and urban, liberal and conservative, I say to you quite frankly that the time for racial discrimination is over. Our people have already made this major and difficult decision, but we cannot underestimate the challenge of hundreds of minor decisions.

". . . No poor, rural, weak or black person should ever have to bear the additional burden of being deprived of the opportunity of an education, a job or simple justice. . . . As governor, I will never shirk this responsibility."

> —January, 1971, Atlanta;
> Carter's inaugural speech
> as governor

"I don't know why everybody is making such a fuss over this (the inaugural). I've been saying the same thing all summer. Then *The New York Times* comes along and acts as if nobody down here ever said anything like that."

—January, 1971, Atlanta

PLAYMATES

"When I was a boy, almost all my playmates were black. We worked in the fields together, and hunted and fished and swam together, but when it was time for church or for school, we went our separate ways, without really understanding why.

"Our lives were dominated by unspoken, unwritten, but powerful rules, rules that were almost never challenged."

—June 1, 1976, Los Angeles; speech at the Martin Luther King Hospital

BIGGEST MISTAKE

(What was your biggest mistake?)

"Oh, back in the late forties I was reluctant to yield to black people their equality of opportunities. I got over that.

"I know black people better than any of the other candidates. Absolutely. I've lived with them, played with them, fished with them and worked with them.

"I've rowed the same boats, hunted birds behind the same dogs and, when civil rights legislation was passed, I didn't have to walk across the street and say, 'Hi, I'm Jimmy Carter. I've been your neighbor for the last 41 years.' I've known black people and they know me."

—February 27, 1976, Boston; interview

WHITE CITIZENS' COUNCIL

"When I came back to Georgia (in the mid-1950s) I was trying to get established in the church and in the school and in work . . . and pressure developed to organize White Citizens' Councils. I didn't feel like it was proper for me to join . . . but it turned out ultimately that I was the only one in Plains who didn't join."

Two town leaders asked him to join but he refused, Carter said.

"They came back with about eight or ten of my customers and they said they thought it was very important that I join the White Citizens Council; that I was hurting myself in the community by not doing so. I told them I really didn't have any intention to join. . . .

"Later, about 30 to 35 people came to see me. They said they'd decided they wanted me to be accepted in the community and they wanted to pay my dues, which I think was $5. . . . I told them I was prepared to leave Plains and that I didn't care about the $5, and I would take the $5 back and I would put it in the commode in the back of my office and flush it, but I wouldn't give the $5 to the White Citizens' Council.

"Several of the men there said there would be a boycott organized against my business. A few of the men in the group stopped trading with me and never came back. But we weathered it all right. I never did join. There was some coolness there around the church, the filling station for awhile.

"I think they finally looked on me as an anachronistic citizen who had come back and had been misled in the Navy, and they would just bear with me until I had gotten reacclimated to South Georgia ways."

—December, 1974, Atlanta; interview

CHURCH

(Carter said the Deacons at the Plains Baptist Church voted in the early 1960s to eject any black who attempted to worship there.)

"I got up and made a speech and told them that I disagreed; that I thought it was an improper thing to do; that it was contrary to the teachings of Christ; that I wished the church wouldn't take any stand on it.

"There were about 250 at the conference and we had six votes for my position—me and my wife, my two sons, my mother and one other man, and there were about 60 votes the other way.

"I guess about 50 people came up to see me (after the meeting) and said they agreed with me but they didn't want to vote. And I thought for awhile about leaving the church, but I decided that wasn't the thing to do."

—December, 1974, Atlanta; interview

30 QUESTIONS

"The first speech ever made in the Georgia Senate, representing the most conservative district in Georgia, was concerning the abolition of 30 questions that we had so proudly evolved as a subterfuge to keep black

107

citizens from voting and which we used with a great deal of smirking and pride for decades or generations ever since the War between the States—questions that nobody could answer in this room, but which were applied to every black citizen that came to the Sumter County Courthouse or Webster County Courthouse and said, 'I want to vote.' I spoke in that chamber, fearful of the news media reporting it back home, but overwhelmed with a commitment to the abolition of that artificial barrier to the rights of an American citizen. I remember the thing that I used in my speech, that a black pencil salesman at the outer door of the Sumter County Courthouse could make a better judgment about who ought to be sheriff than two highly educated professors at Georgia Southwestern College.

"Dr. Martin Luther King Jr., who was perhaps despised by many in this room because he shook up our social structure that benefitted us and demanded simply that black citizens be treated the same as white citizens, wasn't greeted with approbation and accolades by the Georgia Bar Association or the Alabama Bar Association. He was greeted with horror. Still, once that change was made, a very simple but difficult change, no one in his right mind would want to go back to circumstances prior to that juncture in the development of our nation's society.

"I don't want to go on and on—I'm part of it. But the point I want to make to you is that we still have a long way to go."

—May 4, 1974, Athens, Ga.;
Georgia Law Day Speech

POSSIBLE

Civil rights legislation, including the voting rights bill, "made it possible for a southerner like me to stand before you this evening as a serious candidate for president of the United States."

—June 1, 1976, Los Angeles;
speech at the Martin Luther
King Hospital

THE URBAN POOR

(We seem to be heading for a kind of de facto apartheid in America, a geographic separation of the races, with the white middle class moving to the suburbs and poor minority persons concentrated in the cities. What can federal policy do to alleviate this, above all with you as president?)

"I don't see any possibility or advisability of the federal government trying to legislate where people live. . . .

"Several things can be done, obviously the most important of which is to let the people live where they choose, but to let their lives be made better."

—March 29, 1976, New York;
'76 Presidential Forum

ETHNIC PURITY

(Do you favor scattered-site housing for low-income people in the suburbs?)

"I see nothing wrong with ethnic purity being maintained. I would not force a racial integration by government action but I would not permit discrimination against a family moving into a neighborhood."

—April 2, 1976, Milwaukee;
airborne interview

"I have nothing against a community that is made up of people that are Polish, that are Czechoslovakians, who are French-Canadians or who are blacks from trying to maintain the ethnic purity of their neighborhoods. This is a natural inclination on the part of people.

"I made the statement in Milwaukee where there has been over a period of 100 to 150 years a compatibility among neighborhoods where the churches, the private clubs, the newspapers, the restaurants are designed to accommodate the members of a particular ethnic group. I see nothing wrong with that as long as it is done freely. I would never, though, condone any sort of discrimination against, say a black family or another family from moving into that neighborhood.

"But I don't think the government ought to deliberately try to break down an ethnically oriented neighborhood by artificially injecting into it someone from another ethnic group, just to create some sort of integration.

"I was the sponsor of and passed, as governor of Georgia, an open housing bill, which was unheard of in the South, and it passed. The Georgia Legislature supported it, and I made sure we had no carry-over remnants of discrimination against blacks who wanted to move into white neighborhoods on their own volition.

"But I would not have supported a state program to inject black families into a white neighborhood just to create some sort of integration. So the freedom of movement of families into and out of a neighborhood,

I would maintain that, with my own influence as president, and with law. But to artificially inject another ethnic group into a community that was made up primarily of an ethnic group, I would not favor that."

—April 6, 1976, Indianapolis; press conference

"I would like to make any federal housing project first of all under the control of local government—make them compatible with the existing homes. . . .

(Asked about high-rise apartment developments in suburbs . . .)

"If the purpose simply is to create some sort of racial percentage as percentages that destroy the make-up of the neighborhood, I would be reluctant to do that. . . .

"To artificially create within a community that's homogeneous in racial or economic status a diametrically opposite kind of family, I think is bad for the community on both sides. . . ."

(Asked if there is need for affirmative action to integrate housing in the North . . .)

"I can't describe the whole housing program. The only thing I can do is tell you about my experience in Georgia, and if you refuse to let me use the experience I've had it constrains me a great deal in trying to answer your question. . . .

"In Atlanta, for instance, we had rigidly established white neighborhoods and there was an adamant opposition to the intrusion of blacks into those all-white neighborhoods. I pushed, over great difficulty, for the open housing legislation because the federal government particularly under Nixon, was not enforcing the federal open housing standards and this was designed to permit the mixing of the races in the particular neighborhoods if the newcomers prefer to live there. . . .

"There's the purpose of open housing legislation, whether it applies to the South or the North. If you are trying to make something out of nothing, then I resent that effort. I'm not trying to say that I want to maintain with any sort of government interference the ethnic purity of neighborhoods. I do not say that at all.

"What I say is that the government ought not to take as a major purpose the intrusion of alien groups into a neighborhood simply to establish their intrusion. But I don't want to prevent anyone from moving where they choose. I would resist that very strongly and it's much easier to resist that in Cicero (Ill.) than it is in Atlanta. . . .

"The question was would I use a government force to require the intrusion into an ethnically similar neighborhood of groups just because they were different—and my answer was no I would not. I think all of you were at the meeting when I was asked the question. At the time that the question was asked and the question was answered, none of you noticed it. There was nothing notable about it. Now in retrospect you are trying to make something out of it and there's nothing to be made out of it."

(Asked his stand on affirmative action . . .)

That's where I would use the federal government actively to insure that black groups have a chance to live where they please. . . . I set up for the first time a real estate commission in Georgia, with an administrator to guarantee there was an end to blockbusting, to the obstacles placed in the way of black intrusion in the neighborhoods. There has been substantial improvement in the last three years since the law was passed by my administration. There's been a substantial improvement in the ability of blacks to live where they choose. To me that's appalling to say that, because you are black, or because you are Jewish, or because you come from a family that was of Czech parentage, you can't move in here and buy a house if you choose. But to take a neighborhood that's made up of all Czech people and to deliberately try to create with it an enclave of blacks or other groups, simply to try to integrate the neighborhood is contrary to my philosophy and I would not do it. . . .

I'm not insisting on the phrase pure ethnic community. That's not my phrase; that was a question asked of me, and I'm not trying to keep any neighborhood pure."

—April 6, 1976, South Bend;
press conference

"I do want to apologize to all of those concerned for the 'unfortunate' choice of words. It was 'a very serious mistake on my part.' "

(Asked if he had been trying to send a message to white voters opposed to integrated housing . . .)

"No, that is not the case. When I made that statement it was not a predetermined thing."

—April 8, 1976, Philadelphia;
press conference

BUSING

"We have tried in Atlanta mandatory busing. It didn't work. The only kids I have ever bused are poor children. I have never seen a rich child bused. . . .

"This is the plan that we worked out. . . .

"First of all, any child who wants to be bused can be bused at public expense. Secondly, the busing must

113

contribute to increased integration. You can't be bused away from a school just because it's got black kids in it. Third—and this is completely missing in Boston and a lot of other cities, but it's integral for an ultimate solution—the black leaders have to be adequately represented in the decision-making processes of a school system at all levels. . . .

"If federal courts rule differently from what I believe, I will support the federal court. But I believe this is not the subject to be reopened with a constitutional amendment. I would really hate to see that done."

—January 26, 1976; position paper

Carter said he would not oppose the use of segregated private schools "as an escape valve for families who simply cannot bear to have their children go to an integrated school. I wouldn't get in the way of that system."

—February 27, 1976, Boston speech at Faneuil Hall rally

BUSING LIMITS

"I do not believe it would be feasible to put a three-year limit or a five-year limit on a federal court ruling. That would require a constitutional amendment and I don't think that's feasible."

—June 22, 1976, Boston; fundraising reception

VOTING

"Guarantees . . . similar to those provided in the Voting Rights Acts should be extended to all parts of the nation where minority representation and participation are clearly inadequate. . . .

"I also support postcard registration for voting."

—January 26, 1976; position paper

CABINET BLACKS

"When I'm elected there will be black members in my cabinet. You can depend on it."

—April 16, 1976, Washington; speech to religious leaders

9

World Order

SPIRIT

"It is time once again for the world to feel the forward movement and effervescence of a dynamic and confident United States of America."

—June 23, 1976, New York;
speech to Foreign Policy
Association

A PREDICTION FOR THE FALL

"I think that following the convention this year, perhaps as much as at any time in recent history, the debate, if I'm successful, will be between myself and President Ford on foreign policy. I think domestic issues will be much less significant than the debate on basic foreign policy."

—March 25, 1976, Madison, Wisc.; interview

FOREIGN FOCUS

"Our foreign policy is without focus. It is not understood by the people, by the Congress or by foreign nations."

—April 29, 1976; airborne interview

WORLD ORDER

"For too long, our foreign policy has consisted almost entirely of maneuver and manipulation, based on the assumption that the world is a jungle of competing national antagonisms, where military supremacy and economic muscle are the only things that work and where rival powers are balanced against each other to keep the peace. . . .

"Balance of power politics may have worked in 1815, or even 1945, but it has a much less significant role in today's world. Of course there are rivalries— racial religious, national—some of them bitter. But the need for cooperation, even between rivals, goes deeper than all of them."

—March 15, 1976, Chicago; speech to the Council on Foreign Relations

FOREIGN POLICY

"Our (foreign) policies should be as open and honest and decent and compassionate as the American people themselves are. Our policies should be shaped with the participation of Congress, from the outset, on a bi-partisan basis. And they should emerge from broad and well-informed public debate and participation. . . .

"Our policies should treat the people of other nations as individuals, with the same dignity and respect we demand for ourselves. . . .

"It must be the responsibility of the president to restore the moral authority of this country in its conduct of foreign policy. We should work for peace and the control of arms in everything we do. We should support the humanitarian aspirations of the world's people. Policies that strengthen dictators or create refugees, policies that prolong suffering or postpone racial justice weaken that authority."

—March 15, 1976, Chicago; speech to the Council of Foreign Relations

THE FOREIGN VIEW

"The people of other nations have learned, in recent years, that they can sometimes neither trust what our government says nor predict what it will do. They have been hurt and disappointed so many times that they no longer know what to believe about the United States. They want to respect us. They like our people. But our people do not seem to be running our government.

"Every time we have made a serious mistake in recent years in our dealings with other nations, the American people have been excluded from the process of evolving and consumating our foreign policy."

—March 15, 1976, Chicago; speech
to Council on Foreign
Relations

AMBASSADORS

"In the last two or three years, I've traveled as an official visitor to 11 foreign countries, in the Far East, the Mid-East, South America, Central America and Europe, and met with leaders there, and talked to them at length. I've also been to our embassies. . . .

"When I go into an embassy in South America or Central America or Europe and see sitting as our ambassador, our representative there, a fat, bloated, ignorant, rich major contributor to a presidential campaign who can't even speak the language of the country in which he serves, and knows less about our own country and our consciousness and our ideals and our motivation, it's an isult to me and to the people of America and to the people of that country."

—November 23, 1975, Louisville;
Democratic Issues Conference

(Can you name one such fat, ignorant, bloated ambassador who can't speak the language?)

"No, I wouldn't want to name any."

(Can you name one, though?)

"The point I make is that—whether they are actually fat or thin—that they are appointed because there are political interrelationships and not because of quality."

—March 14, 1976, Washington;
CBS's Face the Nation

FOLLY

"Our people have now learned the folly of our trying to inject our power into the internal affairs of other nations. It is time that our government learned that lesson, too."

—June 23, 1976, New York;
speech to the Foreign Policy
Association

NO ACCOMODATION

"East-West relations will be both cooperative and competitive for a long time to come. We want the competition to be peaceful, and we want the cooperation to increase. But we will never seek accomodation at the expense of our own national interests or the interests of our allies."

—June 23, 1976, New York;
speech to the Foreign Policy
Association

DEFENSE

"The prime responsibility of any president is to guarantee the security of our nation, with a tough, muscular, well-organized and effective fighting force. We must have the ability to avoid the threat of successful attack or blackmail and we must always be strong enough to carry out our legitimate foreign policy. This is a prerequisite to peace."

—March 15, 1976, Chicago; speech to Council on Foreign Relations

SCRUTINY

"I guarantee you the defense budget is going to get its first scrutiny in years. . . . We're spending $9 billion a year on weapons we don't need, weapons incompatible with our foreign policy. We've committed ourselves—mind you, a peaceful nation—to the rapid escalation of our nuclear weapons. I think this nation should have as its goal, zero nuclear weapons."

—January 21, 1975, Princeton, N.J.; interview

THE PENTAGON BUDGET

"Without endangering the defense of our nation or our commitments to our allies, we can reduce present defense expenditures by about $5 to $7 billion annually. We must be hard-headed in the development of new weapons systems to assure that they will comport with our foreign policy objectives. Exotic weapons which serve no real function do not contribute to the defense of this country. The B-1 bomber is an example of a proposed system which should not be funded and would be wasteful of taxpayers' dollars. We have an admiral for every 17 ships. The Chief of Naval operations has more captains and commanders on his own personal staff than serve in all the ships at sea.

"The Pentagon bureaucracy is wasteful and bloated.

We have more generals and admirals today than we did during World War II commanding a much smaller fighting force. We can thin our troops in Asia and close some unnecessary bases abroad."

—May, 1976; Carter's
platform presentation

HANDS TIED—DISPUTED

(Do you want to say anything about the Defense budget?)
"I don't want to tie my hands as president. Anyway, there's no political advantage in the issue."

—April 21, 1976, airborne in
Pennsylvania; conversation
with speechwriter; the Carter
campaign denies he ever said
this

ROBERT SHRUM

(Shrum, the speechwriter who quit the campaign)
"Misinterpreted my position on the issues. . . .
"I think he felt that because of his superlative speechwriting he could just deliver a speech to me and I'd parrot it to the public."

—May 3, 1976, Indianapolis;
press conference

SOVIETS—DETENTE

"To the Soviets, detente is an opportunity to continue the process of world revolution without running the threat of a nuclear war."

—May, 1976; Carter's platform
presentation

DETENTE

"I approve of the concept of detente. I don't think we'll have a permanent settlement in the Middle East without the full cooperation of the Soviet Union. Our interests are best served by strengthening cultural exchanges, promoting trade agreements, tourism, student exchange with the Soviet Union. But I would be a tough bargainer. Whenever the Soviet Union derived a benefit from negotiations, I would want to derive an equivalent benefit."

—April 29, 1976; airborne
interview

"I support the objectives of detente but I cannot go along with the way it has been handled by Presidents Nixon and Ford. The secretary of state has tied its success too closely to his personal reputation. As a result, he is giving up too much and asking for too little. He is trumpeting achievements on paper, while failing to insist on them in practice."

—March 15, 1976, Chicago; speech
to the Council on Foreign
Relations

HENRY KISSINGER

Our foreign policy "is primarily comprised of Mr. Kissinger's own ideas, his own goals, most often derived and maintained in secrecy. I don't think the president plays any substantial role in the evolution of our foreign policy. Kissinger has a tendency to neglect our natural allies and friends. . . .

"I think Kissinger still deals in his negotiations on the concept of power blocs. I think we need to deal more directly with individual nations, and to strengthen our bilateral friendships with those nations."

—April 29, 1976; airborne interview

LONE RANGER

"Under the Nixon-Ford Administration, there has evolved a kind of secretive 'Lone Ranger' foreign policy—a one-man policy of international adventure. This is not an appropriate policy for America."

—June 23, 1976, New York; speech to the Foreign Policy Association

FAILED VENTURES

"In every foreign venture that has failed—whether it was Vietnam, Cambodia, Chile, Angola or in the excesses of the CIA—our government forged ahead without consulting the American people, and did things that were contrary to our basic character."

> —March 15, 1976, Chicago; speech to the Council on Foreign Relations

COVERT

"We have learned that we must not use the CIA or other covert means to effect violent change in any government or government policy."

> —May, 1976; Carter's platform presentation

ASSASSINATIONS

"It is . . . un-American to engage in assassinations in time of peace in any country."

> —March 15, 1976, Chicago; speech to Council on Foreign Relations

CIA

"If the CIA ever makes a mistake, I will call a press conference and tell the people. If it ever happens again, I will be responsible."

> —March 10, 1976, Champaign, Ill.; addressing students

STABILITY

"A stable world order cannot become a reality when people of many nations of the world suffer mass starvation, when the countries with capital and technology belligerently confront other nations for the control of raw materials and energy sources, when open and non-discriminatory trade has become the exception rather than the rule; when there are no established arrangements for supplying the world's food and energy, nor for governing control and development of the seas and when there are no effective efforts to deal with population explosions or environmental quality. . . .

"It is likely that, in the future, the issues of war and peace will be more a function of economic and social problems than of the military security problems which have dominated international relations since 1945."

> —March 15, 1976, Chicago; speech
> to the Council on Foreign
> Relations

DEVELOPING NATIONS

"An attitude of neglect and disrespect toward the developing nations of the world is predicated in part on a sense of superiority toward others—a form of racism. This is incompatible with the character of American people."

> —March 15, 1976, Chicago; speech
> to the Council on Foreign
> Relations

"Our participation with developing nations is peripheral and unplaned. We have treated them almost with contempt. A small amount of investment and genuine interest would pay rich dividends. I think the small nations are hungry for a more predictable and mutually advantageous relationship with our country."

—April 29, 1976; airborne
interview

HUMAN NEEDS

"Our program of international aid to developing nations should be redirected so that it meets the minimum human needs of the greatest number of people. This means an emphasis on food, jobs, education and public health—including access to family planning. . . . The time has come to stop taxing poor people in rich countries for the benefit of rich people in poor countries."

—March 15, 1976, Chicago; speech
to the Council on Foreign
Relations

NEGLECT

"We need to reorder our diplomatic priorities. In recent years, we have paid far more attention to our adversaries than to our friends, and we have been especially neglectful of our neighbors in Latin America."

—March 15, 1976, Chicago; speech
to the Council on Foreign
Relations

PROLIFERATION

"There is the fearsome prospect that the spread of nuclear reactors will mean the spread of nuclear weapons to many nations. By 1990, the developing nations alone will produce enough plutonium in their reactors to build 3000 Hiroshima-size bombs a year. . . .

"The reality of this danger was highlighted by the Indian nuclear explosion of May, 1974, which provided a dramatic demonstration that the development of nuclear power gives any country possessing a reprocessing plant a nuclear weapons option."

—May 13, 1976, United Nations; speech

"We Americans must be honest about the problems of proliferation of nuclear weapons. Our nuclear deterrent remains an essential element of world order in this era. Nevertheless, by enjoining sovereign nations to forego nuclear weapons, we are asking for a form of self-denial that we have not been able to accept ourselves.

"I believe we have little right to ask others to deny themselves such weapons for the indefinite future unless we demonstrate meaningful progress toward the goal of control, then reduction, and ultimately elimination of nuclear arsenals."

—May 13, 1976, United Nations; speech

TEST BAN

"There is one step that can be taken at once. The

United States and the Soviet Union should conclude an agreement prohibiting all nuclear explosions for a period of five years, whether they be weapons or so-called 'peaceful' nuclear exposions, and encourage all other countries to join. At the end of the five-year period the agreement can be continued if it serves the interests of the parties."

—May 13, 1976, United Nations; speech

SALT

"It is time, in the SALT talks, that we complete the stage of agreeing on (arms) ceilings and get down to the centerpiece of SALT—the actual negotiation of reductions in strategic forces and measures effectively halting the race in strategic weapons technology. The world is waiting, but not necessarily for long."

—May 13, 1976, United Nations; speech

ARMS SALES

"We and our allies must work together to limit the flow of arms into the developing world. . . .

"As long as the more powerful nations exploit the less powerful, they will be repaid by terrorism, hatred and potential violence. Insofar as our policies are selfish, or cynical, or shortsighted, there will inevitably be a day of reckoning.

"I am particularly concerned by our nation's role as the world's leading arms salesman. . . .

"The fact is that we cannot have it both ways."

—June 23, 1976, New York; speech to the Foreign Policy Association

UNITED NATIONS

"We have all been deeply disturbed by the drift of the United Nations and the other international organizations, and by the acrimony and cliquishness that seems to have taken hold. But it would be a mistake to give up on the United Nations. . . .

"Other countries (should) know in advance the importance the United States attaches to their behavior in the United Nations and other international organizations."

—March 15, 1976, Chicago; speech to the Council on Foreign Relations

NATO

"There is . . . a pressing need for us and our allies to undertake a review of NATO's forces and its strategies in light of the changing military environment.

"A comprehensive program to develop, procure and equip NATO with the more accurate air defense and anti-tank weapons made possible by new technology is needed to increase NATO's defensive power. Agreement on stockpiles and on the prospective length of any potential conflict is necessary. We should also review the structure of NATO reserve forces so they can be committed to combat sooner."

—June 23, 1976, New York; speech to the Foreign Policy Association

TRI-LATERAL

"The time has come for us to seek a partnership between North America, Western Europe and Japan. Our three regions share economic, political and security concerns that make it logical that we should seek ever-increasing unity and understanding."

—June 23, 1976, New York; speech to the Foreign Policy Assoication

ISRAEL

"Rarely in history have two nations been so closely bound together as the United States and Israel. We are both democratic nations, we both cherish freedom of the press, freedom of expression and freedom of religion. We are both nations of immigrants. We both share cultural and artistic values. We are friends and we are constant allies. Ours was the first nation to recognize the state of Israel when it was formed, and we must remain the first nation to which Israel can turn in time of need."

—June 6, 1976, Elizabeth, N.J.; speech at a Jewish center

ZIONISM

"I reject utterly the charge that Zionism is a form of racism. Indeed, Zionism has been in part a response to racism against the Jewish people. . . .

"'The survival of Israel is not a political issue. It is a moral imperative and I would never yield on that point."

—June 6, 1976; Elizabeth N.J., speech at a Jewish Center

MID-EAST

A Mid-east settlement must be based on "a recognition of the right of the Palestinian people . . . and the P.L.O. (Palestine Liberation Army) must recognize the rights of Israel. . . .

"Israel will have to withdraw to the 1967 boundaries."

—December 9, 1975, Medford, Mass.; college address

"Peace in the Middle East depends more than anything else on a basic change in attitude. To be specific, on Arab recognition of the right of Israel to exist as a Jewish state.

"Now this change of attitude on the part of the Arab states must be reflected in tangible and concrete actions including first of all the recognition of Israel, which they have not yet done; secondly, diplomatic relations with Israel; third, a peace treaty with Israel; fourth, open frontiers by Israel's neighbors; last, an end to embargo and official hostile propoganda against the state of Israel."

—June 6, 1976, Elizabeth, N.J.; speech at a Jewish center

"The other principle of the United Nations Resolution 242 calls for, and again I quote, 'Withdrawal of Israel's armed forces from territories occupied in the recent conflict.' This language leaves open the door for changes in the pre-1967 lines my mutual agreement.

"Final borders between Israel and her neighbors should be determined in direct negotiations between the parties and they should not be imposed from outside."

—June 6, 1976, Elizabeth, N.J.; speech at a Jewish center

"There is a humanitarian core within the complexities of the Palestinian problem. Too many human beings, denied a sense of hope for the future, are living in make-shift and crowded camps where demagogues and terrorists can feed on their dispair. They have rights which must be recognized in any settlement and the government of Israel has made it clear that it is sensitive to that fact."

—June 6, 1976, Elizabeth, N.J.; speech at a Jewish center

"Whatever the plight of the Palestinians and whatever may be their hopes for the future, they cannot dictate their agenda by terrorism or war."

—April 1, 1976, New York; policy speech

JEWISH APPEAL

"We have to be cautious. We don't want to offend anybody. . . . I don't want any more statements on the Mideast or Lebanon. Jackson has all the Jews anyway. It doesn't matter how far we go. I don't get over four percent of the Jewish vote anyway, so forget it. We get the Christians."

—April 19, 1976; comment in staff meeting, as quoted by then-speechwriter Robert Shrum. Carter disputes the quotation.

JAPAN

"With regard to our primary Pacific ally, Japan, we will maintain our existing security arrangements, so long as that continues to be the wish of the Japanese people and government."

—June 23, 1976, New York; speech to the Foreign Policy Association

136

KOREA

"I believe it will be possible to withdraw our ground forces from South Korea on a phased basis over a time span to be determined after consultation with both South Korea and Japan. At the same time, it should be made clear to the South Korean government that its internal oppression is repugnant to our people and undermines the support for our comitment there."

—June 23, 1976, New York;
speech to the Foreign Policy
Association

CHINA

"Our relations with China are important to world peace and they directly affect the world balance. The United States has a great stake in a nationally independent, secure and friendly China. The present turmoil in Chinese domestic politics could be exploited by the Soviets to promote a Sino-Soviet reconciliation that might be inimical to international stability and to American interests. I believe that we should explore more actively the possibility of widening American-Chinese trade relations and of further consolidating our political relationships."

—March 15, 1976, Chicago; speech
to the Council on Foreign
Relations

ITALY

"I would certainly hate to see Italy go Communist. I think we ought to do everything we can within reasonable and open bounds through NATO, through our strengthening of the position of the more democratic leaders, to prevent it. As an ultimate thing, though, if it becomes obvious that the present government is incapable of leadership and the Communists are the choice of the people of Italy—which I don't think will occur, by the way—then I don't think we ought to intervene militarily or by any sort of covert means. That would include assassinations, for instance. I don't think that would be right."

—November 23, 1975, Louisville; Democratic Issues Conference

PANAMA

"I would not be in favor of relinquishing actual control or its use to any other nation, including Panama. I think we've got to retain that actual practical control. On the other hand, I think there are several things that can be done to assuage the feeling among the Panamanians that they've been excluded or perhaps even out-traded back in the 1903 period. So I would be glad to yield part of the sovereignty over the Panama Canal Zone to Panama. I would certainly be willing to renegotiate the payment terms to Panama and I would be willing to remove the word 'perpetuity' from the present agreement."

—November 23, 1975, Louisville; Democratic Issues Conference

10

. . . And If Elected

FIRST

"The first piece of legislation I will send to Congress will initiate a complete overhaul of our federal bureaucracy and budgeting systems. By executive order, I will require zero-base budgeting for all federal departments, bureaus and boards.

"The second part, as a follow-up to the first, would initiate the reorganization of our federal bureaucratic structure. I believe the present 1900 federal departments can be reduced to no more than 200, with a great savings in tax money and a streamlining of services to our people."

—January 16, 1976; position paper

SPECIFICS

In 1972, Carter denounced the Nixon Administration for obscuring policies with a "shadow show" and urged Democrats to counter this by cramming their platform with "specifics."

Americans are "fed up with equivocation and superficiality."

> —June, 1972, Washington; testimony to platform committee

"A full-time candidate can't spell out three years ahead of time what specific form the government will take."

> —February 25, 1976, Boston; press conference

BALANCED BUDGET

(Is the idea of a balanced budget out of date now?)

"No. I favor balanced budgets over the business cycle. If the economy is managed progressively, we can attain a balanced budget with full employment by 1979—before the end of the first term of my administration. Putting people to work, don't forget, would enlarge the amount of taxes the government collects and reduce what it spends to fight unemployment."

> —May, 1976; airborne interview

ZERO BASE

"As I traveled around the state of Georgia for four years campaigning for governor I had evolved in my own mind a new budgeting technique which Georgia established which is now used for four years—first time in the world—extremely effective management to be called 'zero base budgeting.' We stripped the Georgia government budget down to zero each year and we start from scratch and we analyze individually every single program we have in Georgia. If it's a good program, we keep it. If it has served its purpose, it's abolished. If it needs improving, we'll mend it."

—March 20, 1975, San Francisco;
speech at civic club

REVENUE SHARING

"I would favor an approach that would give funds directly to local cities and communities rather than the states. . . . It is a means of giving local governments more control over programs that affect them daily. . . . Second, and more important, local communities do not have the capacity to generate extra income —through taxes or other methods—that the states have."

—January 26, 1976; position paper

FORD'S ECONOMY

"I think there's a very good likelihood that we'll have roughly seven precent inflation and seven percent unemployment in November. If it's better than that, it can't be attributed to any action on the part of (President) Ford."

—April 29, 1976; airborne
interview

INFLATION VS. JOBS

"I think the Conference Board has indicated—a very distinguished group, I think you'd agree—that if we put a major emphasis on employment, that the inflation rate would increase very slightly. And I don't know what the figure would be, but I would place a major emphasis on employment and take my chances with inflation, if I had to."

—February 23, 1976, Boston; Presidential Forum

TAXES

"Our national tax system is a disgrace. The income most certain to be taxed is that which is derived from manual labor. . . .

"A piecemeal approach to change will not work. Basically, I favor a simplified tax system which treats all income the same, taxes all income only once, and makes our system of taxation more progressive."

—May, 1976; platform presentation

HOMEOWNER DEDUCTIONS

"We must undertake a comprehensive review of the hidden ways in which our tax laws influence housing policy. Deductible mortgage interest and property taxes benefit upper- and middle-income homeowners in the amount of $11 billion, while total federal

143

expeditures for subsidized housing amount to approximately $2 billion."

—January 26, 1976; position paper

(Do you favor the repeal of tax loopholes like, one, interest and property tax deductions on homes, depreciation on apartment projects and investment credits on construction machinery to build houses and apartments?)

"I'll come out with a complete analysis of our tax system later on this year, I hope. But in general I would say, along with the elimination of hundreds of other tax incentives, those would be among those that I would like to do away with. I think that we need to come out in this country with a comprehensive, all-inclusive tax reform bill. I don't think it will ever come from the Congress. I'm not being critical of the Congress. But it's too complicated and too important to ever do piecemeal.

"In 1913, I think it was, when the income tax laws were passed, or when the Constitution was amended to permit income tax, we envisioned a structure, with all income treated the same, with income being taxed only once, with a truly progressive tax rate, so that those who made the most income per year paid a higher percentage of their income in total taxes, and with a very minimum of tax incentives or loopholes.

"So, the answer would be, back to those three particular instances, yes, but it would include a lot of others that would also be eliminated.

"Now, if we can simplify our tax structure, which I propose to do as president, I believe the American people and the Congress would go along with it. But it's got to be the elimination of a lot of incentives and not just those particular three that you named."

—February 23, 1976, Boston; Presidential Forum

"I will seriously consider the abolition of all (deductions, including the homeowner benefits.)
This would be part of an overall reform that would "reduce the tax rate by 40 to 50 percent and shift the tax load to those with higher incomes."

—February 27, 1976, Boston; rally

"I want to point out this thing about homeowners getting exemptions on property taxes paid and interest payments made. Those two factors cost the government about $10 billion, which is good, because I favor having that much money go into letting families own their own homes. But you've got a problem with it, because half of that money . . . about $5 billion, goes to only 15 percent of homeowners, the ones that are in the higher income brackets. This is a very important consideration. Now, if you've got $10 billion to spend to encourage families to own their own homes, who ought to get the money? Who ought to get the savings? The people that need it most. But if a person's in a 70 percent income tax bracket, that provision pays 70 percent of their interest on their mortgages. If a person's in a 20 percent income tax bracket, that provision only pays 20 percent of their interest on their home mortgage. So, that's an upside-down proposition. And I would rather see that $10 billion spent, yes, to help homeowners, but to go to those families who have the low and medium incomes, not to the rich people.

"One other thing I want to say is I believe that that provision also applies to families for their second homes and their vacation homes and their summer homes. Well, most people in this country don't own two or three houses and most people in this country don't make over $25,000 a year. So I want to see those savings go to people who need it most, for a change."

—March 1, 1976, Miami;
'76 Presidential Forum

TAX REFORM

(Asked to explain a recent modification of his proposal to eliminate mortgage interest deductions as part of a sweeping tax reform.)

"I don't really have the capability or the inclination at this point to elaborate or describe the specifics. . . . (And) I don't have time to study it."

—March 11, 1976, Chicago;
press conference

MULTINATIONALS

"We need too . . . remove all incentives that have encouraged our multinational corporations, or American corporations, to manufacture products in foreign

146

countries when our own employees in this country are out of work. That may have been okay five, ten, fifteen years ago, when employment was high, but it's not okay any more. And I've been in Germany recently, and you see General Motors plants, Chrysler plants, Ford plants all over Germany. You never see any Volkswagen plants in this country, and you won't see any until Germany either runs out of labor or until the ratio between the mark and the dollar in value becomes to their advantage to manufacture products over here."

—February 23, 1976, Boston;
Presidential Forum

PRIORITY

"The first priority must be a rapid reduction of unemployment and the achievement of full employment with price stability. For the near future, economic policy should be expansionary. By 1979, we can achieve a balanced budget within the context of full employment."

—May, 1976; platform presentation

JOBS

"I'm not in favor of solving our major unemployment problems simply by creating government jobs. Somebody's got to pay those salaries, and I don't see anybody to pay those salaries except people who work outside the government and pay taxes. . . .

147

"I would certainly create federal jobs in some categories, say young people, where the unemployment rate is so high, as Congressman (Morris) Udall pointed out, 40-45 percent among minority young people. But before I would do that, I would rather invest part of our federal monies into industries that have to cut back on employment."

—February 23, 1976, Boston;
Presidential Forum

WELFARE

"No person on welfare should earn more than the working poor can earn at their jobs.

"Strong work incentives, job creation and job training should be provided. . . .

"Family stability should be encouraged. . . .

"Persons who are legitimately on welfare should be treated with respect and dignity. . . .

"The 1.3 million people drawing welfare who are able to work full-time should be taken out of the welfare system; they should be trained for a job and offered a job. If they decline a job, they should be ineligible for further benefits.

"The welfare burden should be removed from cities, with all welfare costs being paid by the federal and state governments. . . .

"To achieve these goals, I propose one fairly uniform, nationwide payment, varying according to cost-of-living differences between communities. It should be funded in substantial part by the federal government with strong work and job incentives for the poor who are employable and with income supplementation for the working poor, and with earnings tied so

148

as to encourage employment, so that it would never be more profitable to stay on welfare than to work."

—May, 1976; platform presentation

WELFARE MOTHERS

"I achieved welfare reform by opening up 136 day-care centers for the retarded and using welfare mothers to staff them. Instead of being on welfare, these thousand of women now have jobs and self-respect. You should see them bathing and feeding the retarded children. They're the best workers we have in the state government."

—December, 1975, Mississippi; at a house party.

HEALTH

"We need a national health insurance program, financed by general tax revenues and employer-employee shared payroll taxes, which is universal and mandatory. Such a program must reduce barriers to preventive care, provide for uniform standards and reforms in the health care delivery system, and assure freedom of choice in the selection of physicians and treatment centers.

"We must shift our emphasis in both private and public health care away from hospitalization and acute-care services to preventive medicine and the early detection of the major cripplers and killers of the American people. . . .

"Another major problem is to better utilize the health personnel available to us."

—May, 1976; platform
presentation

CITIES

"More than 40 years ago, President Franklin Roosevelt declared that America's No. 1 economic problem was poverty in the South. President Roosevelt was right and he had the vision and the political ability to enact (rural public works and electrification) programs . . . that changed my life and the lives of millions of people living in the South.

"Today, America's No. 1 economic problem is our cities, and I want to work with you to meet the problem of urban America just as Franklin Roosevelt worked to meet the problems of the rural South in the '30s."

—June 29, 1976, Milwaukee;
mayors' conference

GUARANTEEING BONDS

"If we guarantee city bonds or state bonds . . . somebody's got to guarantee the purchaser of those bonds that the budget will be managed properly and balanced in the cities and states. . . .

"I wouldn't favor guaranteeing of the cities' bonds or the state bonds until they meet the same requirements of integrity and proof that the bonds will be sound as are required in the corporate world. And if the bonds are guaranteed, they ought not to be tax-free."

—March 29, 1976, New York;
'76 Presidential Forum

HOUSING

"A direct subsidy of new housing units is essential in order to construct new low- and middle-income housing and to stimulate the construction industry. We should work toward providing low-income citizens with an adequate housing allowance. . . .

"We must let local authorities, with their experience and knowledge, produce and maintain low-income housing. . . .

"There should be federal guarantees to prevent red-lining in urban neighborhoods. . . .

"We must provide a steady supply of credit for the housing industry to minimize the boom-and-bust roller-coaster which presently afflicts the industry."

—January 26, 1976; position paper

EDUCATION

"A major overhaul of the revenue sharing concept is needed. Funds for local governments should be greatly increased and the prohibition against using these funds for education should be eliminated. The federal share of public education costs was 10 percent in 1974. If existing inequalities are to be eliminated and American teachers provided with a decent standard of living, the portion must be increased. . . .

"I will not be hesitant to propose and support basic and controversial changes. . . . Such a program would assure . . . expanded vocational and career education opportunities, the education rights of the handicapped, a stronger voice for education at the federal level through the creation of a separate Department of Education. . . .

"For 14 million citizens of the wealthiest nation in the world to be illiterate is a crime. The still inadequate salaries for thousands of American teachers is equally inexcusable."

—January 16, 1976;
position paper

SOCIAL SECURITY

"I think to increase the income that would be permitted (to a Social Security recipient without losing benefits) by, say, another $1000 to about $3600, would be the best first step. . . .

"I would like to keep the Social Security system separate (from general revenues) and let it be a retirement payment for those who've worked and earned a place in it. That, to me, is a very important psychological difference. And I would much prefer to tax higher levels of income, up to, say, $20-to-$22,000, than to start taking money out of the general fund."

—March 1, 1976, Miami;
'76 Presidential Forum

AMNESTY

"When I am president, I am going to issue a blanket pardon for all those who are outside our country, or

152

in this country, who did not serve in the armed forces. I am going to issue a pardon not an amnesty. There is not much difference; there wouldn't be any punishment. I think those kids who have lived in Sweden or in Canada or have avoided arrest have been punished enough. I think it is time to get it over with.

"In my opinion, amnesty says what you did was right. Pardon says whether what you did was right or wrong, you are forgiven for it. Where I live, most of the young people who were drafted are poor or black. They didn't know where Canada was, they didn't know where Sweden was, they didn't have enough money to hide in college. They went to Vietnam. Some of them came back; a lot of them didn't. And I personally have had a hard time coming to the pardon thing, I'll have to be frank with you. It's just hard for me to equate what the young people did who went and hid in Sweden with what the young men did who went to Vietnam thinking it was a bad war, but who gave their lives for it. And I'd like to draw that subtle distinction to assuage my own conscience."

—January 26, 1967; position paper

DESERTERS

Carter accepted language in the Democratic platform that deserters—as distinct from draft resisters—would be treated "on a case-by-case basis."

—June, 1976

WATERGATE PARDONS?

(Would you consider pardoning Watergate defendandts in prison or awaiting sentence?)

"I don't think it would be appropriate for me to say anything on the subject of Watergate pardons."

—April 29, 1976; airborne
interview

WOMEN'S RIGHTS

"I support the efforts of women to achieve equality through court action when that is required. As a further aid to working women, I support the concept of flexible hours for full-time employees. . . .

"We must insure that we do not demean the roles of homemaker and rearer of children. I firmly believe that there is no higher calling for a man or woman than the care of the children they bring into the world. . . .

"The media too frequently portray women in an inaccurate, belittling manner. More women must be appointed to the Board of Governors of the Public Broadcasting System, the Federal Communications Commission and the Federal Trade Commission. . . .

"As president, I would ensure that . . . social security laws be revised so that women would no longer be penalized."

—January 26, 1976; position paper

E.R.A.

"I strongly support the equal rights amendment. I have campaigned extensively in all 50 states. In every

154

state, I have consistently and unhesitatingly advocated passage of the amendment, and in several states I have voluntarily chaired discussions of the E.R.A.

—February, 1976; questionnaire
in the *New Hampshire Times*

ABORTION

"I've always felt conservative about abortion. I think abortion is wrong and government shouldn't do anything to encourage it."

But any legislation should be "within the confines of the Supreme Court ruling."

—February 1, 1976, Concord, Mass.;
interview

"Without knowing the specifics at this time, I might support a federal statute minimizing abortions beyond the first 13 weeks of pregnancy."

—February, 1976; questionnaire
in the *New Hampshire Times*

OIL

"I suppose restrictions on the right of a single company to own all phases of production and distribution of oil. . . .

"I support legal prohibitions against ownership of competing types of energy, oil and coal for example."

—January 16, 1976; paid ad in the
Des Moines Register

"I think I'm the only Democratic candidate who hasn't called for divestiture of the oil companies."

—April 20, 1976, Houston;
speech to campaign workers

OFFSHORE OIL

"The unrestrained and profuse off-shore leasing of scarce and very lightly understood oil reserves is in no way protecting the public's interest and the public's oil deposits."

—March 15, 1976, Pittsburgh;
speech to National Wildlife
Federation

"I believe we can have adequate energy development along with strict environmental standards; there is no contradiction.

"There are some limitations and policies, however, that must be followed with respect to offshore drilling. There are obviously some places where drilling must not take place. Where it does, we must ensure that strict controls are enforced. Federal officials should accept the states' recommendations regarding lease sales and development plans, unless the officials be-

156

lieve that those recommendations seriously conflict with national security."

—February 11, 1976; response to questions in *New Hampshire Times*

ENERGY POLICY

" 'Project Independence' is a farce. No substantial steps have been taken. . . .

"It is unlikely that we will be totally 'independent' of oil imports during this century. It is certainly not possible or necessary for us to be energy independent by 1985, but we should be free from possible blackmail or economic disaster which might be caused by another boycott. Our reserves should be developed, imports reduced to manageable levels, standby rationing procedures evolved and authorized, and aggressive economic reprisals should await any boycotting oil supplier."

—January 26, 1976; position paper

"I favor a quota system that would keep (oil) imports at the present 40 percent level. . . . The price of all domestic oil should be kept beneath that of OPEC oil.

"We should place the importation of oil under government authority to allow strict control of purchases and the auctioning of purchase orders. Anti-trust laws must be rigidly enforced. Maximum disclosure of data on reserve supplies and production must be required. Unnecessary electrical plant construction should be stopped. Advertising at consumers' expense to encourage increased consumption of electricity should be prohibited. . . .

"We must exploit the potential of solar energy in the construction of new homes and offices.

"The federal government with all its agencies should set a national example in the conservation and proper use of energy."

—January 26, 1976; position paper

ENERGY

"The United States must shift from oil to coal, taking care about the environmental problems involved in coal production and use."

—May 13, 1976, United Nations; speech

SOLAR ENERGY

"I don't think that solar energy is a major panacea for the future, but it's certainly a new kind of energy waiting to be created and used in this country. And small amounts of research and development funds there would provide large numbers of jobs, mostly in New England, I should think, for the design, manufacture, transportation and later the maintenance of solar heating units."

—February 23, 1976, Boston; Presidential Forum

NUCLEAR POWER

"U.S. dependence on nuclear power should be kept to the minimum necessary to meet our needs."

—May 13, 1976, United Nations; speech

"We must maintain the strictest possible safety standards for our atomic power plants, and be completely honest with our people concerning any problems or dangers.

"For instance, nuclear reactors should be located below ground level. The power plants should be housed in sealed buildings within which permanent heavy vacuums are maintained. Plants should be located in sparsely populated areas and only after consultation with state and local officials. Designs should be standardized. And a fulltime federal employee, with full authority to shut down the plant in case of any operational abnormality, should always be present in control rooms."

—January 29, 1976; position paper

ARABS

"I would let the Arab countries know that we want to be their friend, that we are heavily dependent on oil imported from them.

However, the United States should make it clear that "if they declare an embargo against us, we would consider not a military but an economic declaration of war."

—November 30, 1975, Washington; Meet the Press

COLLECTIVE BARGAINING

(Do you believe in comprehensive collective bargaining for all employees, including governmental?)

"Yes, but I favor arbitration for public safety employees."

—January 26, 1976; position paper

RIGHT TO WORK

"I stated during my campaign that I was not in favor of doing away with the right to work law, and that is the position I still maintain."

—January, 1971; letter to the
National Right to Work Committee

"I never cared about right to work one way or another. . . . If you get it through (repealing legislation), I'll sign it."

—February 17, 1976, Boston;
interview

"I think the 14-B should be repealed, which would permit the abolition of right-to-work laws. And if the Congress passes such legislation, I'd be glad to sign it."

—early April, 1976, Waukesha,
Wisc.

ENVIRONMENTAL

"The Democratic Party should . . . hold fast against efforts to lower clean air requirements of the Clean Air Act . . . and . . .

"Encourage the development of rapid transit systems that will help alleviate somewhat our continued and increased dependence on the automobile . . . and . . .

"Protect against the noise pollution with which our advanced technology challenges us. I opposed development of the SST on this basis, and I also opposed granting landing rights to the Concorde."

—May, 1976; platform presentation

AGRICULTURE

"The greatest need among those in the agricultural economy of this nation is a coherent, predictable and stable government policy relating to the production of food and fiber. . . .

"We should again maintain a predictable, reasonably small and stable reserve of agricultural products. About a two months supply would be adequate, with about one-half of these reserves being retained under the control of farmers to prevent government 'dumping' during times of moderate price increases."

—January 16, 1976; position paper

CRIME CONTROL

"The federal government can provide a model for the states by revising our system of sentencing, eliminating much of the discretion given to judges and probation officers, insuring greater certainty in sentencing and confinement, and insuring a higher percentage of serious criminals being imprisoned."

—May, 1976; platform presentation

CAPITAL PUNISHMENT

(What are your views on capital punishment?)
"I favor retention of capital punishment."

—November 1, 1970; pre-election questions in the *Atlanta Constitution*

"I do not believe at this time society can afford the use of the death penalty. I do believe that this is a deterrent, especially in certain cases such as the murder of a prison guard by someone already under life sentence."

Carter added that he would be "personally reluctant to impose the death penalty."

—May 3, 1971, Atlanta

LEGALIZED GAMBLING

(What is your position on legalized gambling?)
"I'm opposed to legalized gambling."

—November 1, 1970; pre-election questions in the *Atlanta Constitution*

NATIONAL GUARD

Carter said that, in a riot, he would authorize the National Guard to . . .

". . . take whatever action is necessary to protect innocent lives, including shoot-to-kill orders, if that is necessary as a last resort to restore order. . . .

"I will not permit disruptions in our cities and on our college campuses."

—October 26, 1970, Valdosta, Ga.;
press conference

HANDGUN CONTROL

"I favor registration of handguns, a ban on the sale of cheap handguns, reasonable licensing provisions, including a waiting period and prohibition of ownership by anyone convicted of a crime involving a gun and by those not mentally competent."

—January 26, 1976; position paper

CRIMINALS

"I don't know, it may be that poor people are the only ones who commit crimes, but I do know they are the only ones who serve prison sentences."

—May 4, 1974, Athens, Ga.;
Georgia Law Day speech

CONVICTS

"Now the thrust of the entire (prisons) program
. . . is to try to discern in the soul of each convicted
and sentenced person, redeeming features that can be
enhanced."

—May 4, 1974, Athens, Ga.;
Georgia Law Day speech

MARIJUANA

"I favor a modified form of marijuana decriminali-
zation, along the lines of the Oregon law which has
civil penalties for small amounts of possesion. I feel
that this legislation should be left up to the individual
states themselves."

—February, 1976; questionnaire
in the *New Hampshire Times*

SUNSHINE LAW

"We need first of all to strip away the secrecy that
surrounds government and to pass an all-inclusive sunshine law to require the deliberations of executive and
legislative committees to be open to the public, to let
the people of this country know what goes on in their
government. . . . It's like a potential source of a cancer
to let a regulatory agency meet and decide mine and
your business behind locked doors."

—April 16, 1975, Misenheimer,
N.C.; speech to college
students

GOVERNMENT FILES

"Broad public access, consonant with the right of personal privacy, should be provided to government files. Maximum security declassification must be implemented."

—May, 1976; platform presentation

ATTORNEY GENERAL

"The attorney general ought to be completely removed from politics. . . . We ought to keep the attorney general, but let him have the full prerogatives and authority and independence that Mr. Jaworski had, to be appointed by the president, yes, and with the confirmation of the Senate, but for a certain period of time not to be removed from office unless the attorney general is guilty of malfeasance."

—April 16, 1975, Misenheimer, N.C.; speech to college students

THE $42,500 CONTRACT

"I don't think any salary increase for the Congress should ever go into effect during that session of Congress. If Congress wants to vote themselves a salary increase, they ought to face the voters before they get the salary increase. To me, when you run for office for two years or four years, it's a contract with the people. I agree to go and serve for four years, two years or six years for $42,500."

—March, 1976, Wisconsin; press conference

LOBBYIST DISCLOSURE

"The deliberations of lobbyists ought to be stripped bare of concealment. We've got a lobbying bill in Congress that is a joke. Every quarter we ought to file a report on expenditures of lobbyists, anything that costs over $250 total for the whole quarter ought to be revealed. How did they spend their money, and why, and to whom?"

—April 16, 1975, Misenheimer, N.C.;
speech to college students

POLITICAL JUDGES

"Should a federal judge be appointed because of past political support for the president? A person who is ultimately responsible for the administration of justice among Democrats, Republicans, Independents, poor people, rich people? It is obvious that federal judges, district attorneys, Supreme Court justices ought to be appointed on the basis of merit and ability and sound judgment and common sense and judicial temperament—not on the basis of politics."

—April 16, 1975, Misenheimer, N.C.;
speech to college students

"Independent blue-ribbon judicial selection committees should be utilized to provide recommendations to the president when vacancies occur, from which the president must make a selection."

—May, 1976; platform presentation

166

THE ISSUE IS PRIVILEGE

"In general, the powerful and the influential in our society shape the laws and have a great influence on the legislature or the Congress. This creates a reluctance to change because the powerful and the influential have carved out for themselves or have inherited a privileged position in society, of wealth or social prominence or higher education or opportunity for the future."

—May 4, 1974, Athens, Ga.;
Georgia Law Day speech

THE ISSUE IS OUTSIDERS

"I can tell you that there is a major and fundamental issue taking shape in this election year. That issue is the division between the 'insiders' and the 'outsiders.' I have been accused of being an outsider. I plead guilty. Unfortunately, the vast majority of Americans—like almost everyone in this room—are also outsiders."

—February 17, 1976, Boston;
speech at rally

ISSUES

"Issues exist in the minds of the people. I don't think a candidate can contrive issues and say that this is the kind of issue I want to run on."

—April 11, 1975, Little Rock;
press conference

Acknowledgments

CHAPTER 1

Running—*New York Times,* January 5, 1975; story by Christopher Lydon

Fear—*Boston Globe,* March 1, 1976; column by Mike Barnicle

Priorities—*The New Yorker,* May 31, 1976; story by Elizabeth Drew

Deciding to Run—*New York Times,* January 5, 1975; story by Christopher Lydon

Doubts—text of Public Broadcasting interview with Bill Moyers

Winning—*Atlanta Constitution,* June 21, 1970; interview with Bill Shipp

Losing—text of Public Broadcasting interview with Bill Moyers

Show Me—*Why Not the Best?* by Jimmy Carter, © Copyright 1975, by Boardman Press, Nashville, Tenn. Used by permission.

Won-Loss Record—*Atlanta Constitution,* February 10, 1971; story by Hal Hayes

New Hampshire-2—*Newsweek,* March 8, 1976

The Liberals—*The New Yorker,* May 31, 1976; story by Elizabeth Drew

Unaccustomed As I Am . . .—New York *Daily News,* May 26, 1976; story by Michael Pousner

Factory Gates—text of Public Broadcasting interview by Bill Moyers

The Press—tape of interview with Curtis Wilkie of *The Boston Globe*

CHAPTER 2

The South—*Why Not the Best?* by Jimmy Carter, © Copyright 1975 by Broadman Press, Nashville, Tenn. Used by permission.

4 a.m.—*Harper's,* March, 1976; story by Steven Brill

Tennis—*Why Not the Best?* by Jimmy Carter, © Copyright 1975, by Broadman Press, Nashville, Tenn. Used by permission.

The Old Submariner—*Atlanta Constitution,* May 4, 1971; story by Bill Shipp

Sports Fan—*Atlanta Constitution,* February 10, 1971; story by Hal Hayes

Tooth Delay—*Why Not the Best?* by Jimmy Carter, © Copyright 1975, by Broadman Press, Nashville, Tenn. Used by permission.

Sucker Fish—*Why Not the Best?* by Jimmy Carter, © Copyright 1975, by Broadman Press, Nashville, Tenn. Used by permission.

No Sweetheart—*Why Not the Best?* by Jimmy Carter, © Copyright 1975, by Broadman Press, Nashville, Tenn. Used by permission.

Ensign—*Why Not the Best?* by Jimmy Carter, ©

CHAPTER 3

Ambition—*Time,* May 10, 1976

Labels—*New York Times,* March 13, 1976; story by Frank Lynn

Labels-2—*Boston Globe,* January 24, 1971; story by Bill Shipp of the *Atlantic Constitution*

Redneck—Atlanta Constitution, June 21, 1970; story by Bill Shipp

A Letter—Disputed—*Harper's,* March, 1976; story by Steven Brill

Talking Down—*The New Republic,* June 26, 1976; story by Robert Coles

A Complaint—*Atlanta Constitution,* June 21, 1970; story by Bill Shipp

Left Out—*Atlanta Journal,* April 7, 1970; story by Steve Ball Jr.

Georgia Busing-1—*Atlanta Constitution,* February 17, 1972; story by Beau Cutts

Humphrey-Wallace—*Atlanta Journal,* June 8, 1972; story by David Nordan

CHAPTER 4

My Opponents—*Madison Times,* March 29, 1976

Combative—*Trenton Times,* February 1, 1976; interview with Wilson Barto

Picking Vice Presidents—*Boston Phoenix,* June 29, 1976; story by James Barron and Marjorie Arons

Other Candidates—New York *Daily News,* May 24, 1976; story by Michael Pousner

Henry Jackson—*Atlanta Constitution,* August 4, 1975; interview by Bill Shipp

Jerry Brown—*Boston Globe,* May 13, 1976; story by Martin F. Nolan

Birch Bayh—*Atlanta Constitution,* August 4, 1975; story by Bill Shipp

Lloyd Bentsen—*Atlanta Constitution,* August 4, 1975; interview with Bill Shipp

Morris Udall—*Atlanta Constitution,* August 4, 1975; story by Bill Shipp

Fred Harris—*New Times,* June 11, 1976; story by Robert Shrum

Ted Kennedy—*Atlanta Journal;* story by David Nordan

George Wallace—*New York Times,* December 14, 1975; story by Patrick Anderson

George Wallace-2—*New York Times,* December 14, 1975; story by Patrick Anderson

Past Southern Candidates—*Washington Star,* January 26, 1975; story by Jack Germond

Sen. Adlai Stevenson—*New Times,* June 11, 1976; story by Robert Shrum

Maynard Jackson—*New Times,* June 11, 1976; story by Robert Shrum

Gerald Ford—*Atlanta Constitution,* August 4, 1975; interview with Bill Shipp

Blame It On. . . —*Boston Globe,* May 9, 1976; story by Curtis Wilkie

CHAPTER 5

Aggressive—*Time,* May 10, 1976
Watergate—*Capital Times,* March 29, 1976

CHAPTER 6

God's Will—text of Public Broadcasting interview by Bill Moyers

A Great Christian—text of Public Broadcasting interview by Bill Moyers

Golden Rule—*Why Not the Best?* by Jimmy Carter, © Copyright 1975, by Broadman Press, Nashville, Tenn. Used by permission.

Second Coming—*Boston Herald,* April 11, 1976; story by Kingsbury Smith of Hearst Newspapers

Exalting Ourselves—*Why Not the Best?* by Jimmy Carter, © Copyright 1975, by Broadman Press, Nashville, Tenn. Used by permission.

Sacrifice—*Time,* May 10, 1976

Born Again—*The New Yorker,* May 31, 1976; story by Elizabeth Drew

Questioning the Bible—*Time,* May 10, 1976

Jimmy's Will—*Washington Post,* March 21, 1976; story by Myra MacPherson

CHAPTER 7

Testing—*Why Not the Best?* by Jimmy Carter, © Copyright 1975, by Broadman Press, Nashville, Tenn. Used by permission.

Courtliness—Tape of interview with Curtis Wilkie of the *Boston Globe*

Quiet—*Boston Globe,* March 1, 1976; column by Mike Barnicle

Compromise—text of Public Broadcasting interview by Bill Moyers

Turtle—*Why Not the Best?* by Jimmy Carter, © Copyright 1972, by Broadman Press, Nashville, Tenn. Used by permission.

Insinuation—tape of interview with Curtis Wilkie of the *Boston Globe*.

Quit?—text of Public Broadcasting interview with Bill Moyers

Books—*Madison Times*, March 29, 1976

Poetry—*Madison Times*, March 29, 1976

Pop—*Madison Times*, March 29, 1976

Classical—*Madison Times*, March 29, 1976

Kids' TV—*The* (Boston) *Real Paper*, February 25, 1976; story by Andy Merton

TV NO—*Madison Times*, March 29, 1976

Pre-marital Affairs—*New York Times*, December 14, 1975; story by Patrick Anderson

Extra-marital affairs—United Press International, June 2, 1976

Legislating Morals—*The* (Boston) *Real Paper*, February 25, 1976; story by Andy Merton

Shucks—*Boston Globe*, March 1, 1976; column by Mike Barnicle

CHAPTER 8

Biggest Mistake—*Boston Globe*, March 1, 1976; column by Mike Barnicle

Race-2—*Boston Globe*, January 24, 1971; story by Bill Shipp of the *Atlanta Constitution*.

CHAPTER 9

A Prediction for the Fall—*Capital Times*, March 29, 1976

Foreign Focus—*Time*, May 10, 1976; interview with Dean E. Fischer. Reprinted by permission from

TIME, The Weekly Newsmagazine; copyright Time Inc.

Scrutiny—*Trenton Times,* February 1, 1975; interview with Wilson Barto

Hands Tied—*New Times,* June 11, 1976; story by Robert Shrum

Detente—*Time,* May 10, 1976; interview with Dean E. Fischer. Reprinted by permission from TIME, The Weekly Newsmagazine; copyright Time Inc.

Henry Kissinger—*Time,* May 10, 1976; interview with Dean E. Fischer. Reprinted by Permission from TIME, The Weekly Newsmagazine; copyright Time Inc.

Developing Nations-2—*Time,* May 10, 1976; interview with Dean E. Fischer. Reprinted by permission from TIME, The Weekly Newsmagazine; copyright Time Inc.

Jewish Appeal—from an unpublished memo of Shrum's. A virtually identical account by Shrum was published in *New Times*

CHAPTER 10

Balanced Budget—*U.S. News and World Report,* May 24, 1976; interview with John Mashek

Ford's Economy—*Time,* May 10, 1976; interview with Dean E. Fischer. Reprinted by permission from TIME, The Weekly Newsmagazine; copyright Time Inc.

Welfare Mothers—*Harper's,* March, 1976; story by Steven Brill. Carter's staff has conceded that the number of welfare mothers in this program is actually in the hundreds.

Watergate Pardons?—*Time,* May 10, 1976; interview with Dean E. Fischer. Reprinted by permission from TIME, The Weekly Newsmagazine; copyright Time Inc.

Abortion—*Boston Globe,* February 2, 1976; story by Curtis Wilkie

Abortion-2—*New Hampshire Times,* February 11, 1976

Arabs—Associated Press, December 1, 1975

Right to Work-3—*Atlanta Constitution,* April 14, 1976; story by Jim Merriner

National Guard—United Press International, October 27, 1970

These books? Fiction.
Keep telling yourself that as you read.

Here are the facts.
The conclusions are up to you.

We know you don't read just one kind of book. | That's why we've got all kinds of bestsellers.